Hoodoo for Beginners

An Essential Guide to Folk Magic and Using African American Spiritual Practice to Enhance Your Life

© Copyright 2023 - All rights reserved.

The content contained within this book may not be reproduced, duplicated, or transmitted without direct written permission from the author or the publisher.

Under no circumstances will any blame or legal responsibility be held against the publisher, or author, for any damages, reparation, or monetary loss due to the information contained within this book, either directly or indirectly.

Legal Notice:

This book is copyright protected. It is only for personal use. You cannot amend, distribute, sell, use, quote, or paraphrase any part, or the content within this book, without the consent of the author or publisher.

Disclaimer Notice:

Please note the information contained within this document is for educational and entertainment purposes only. All effort has been executed to present accurate, up-to-date, reliable, and complete information. No warranties of any kind are declared or implied. Readers acknowledge that the author is not engaging in the rendering of legal, financial, medical, or professional advice. The content within this book has been derived from various sources. Please consult a licensed professional before attempting any techniques outlined in this book.

By reading this document, the reader agrees that under no circumstances is the author responsible for any losses, direct or indirect, that are incurred as a result of the use of the information contained within this document, including, but not limited to, errors, omissions, or inaccuracies.

Free Bonus from Silvia Hill available for limited time

Hi Spirituality Lovers!

My name is Silvia Hill, and first off, I want to THANK YOU for reading my book.

Now you have a chance to join my exclusive spirituality email list so you can get the ebooks below for free as well as the potential to get more spirituality ebooks for free! Simply click the link below to join.

P.S. Remember that it's 100% free to join the list.

~~$27~~ **FREE BONUSES**

 9 Types of Spirit Guides and How to Connect to Them

 How to Develop Your Intuition: 7 Secrets for Psychic Development and Tarot Reading

 Tarot Reading Secrets for Love, Career, and General Messages

Access your free bonuses here
https://livetolearn.lpages.co/hoodoo-for-beginners-paperback/

Table of Contents

INTRODUCTION 1
CHAPTER 1: WHAT IS HOODOO? 3
CHAPTER 2: HOODOO DEITIES AND SPIRITS 8
CHAPTER 3: INGREDIENTS AND MATERIALS YOU NEED 20
CHAPTER 4: GETTING READY FOR HOODOO............................ 33
CHAPTER 5: CREATE A HOODOO SHRINE 43
CHAPTER 6: HOODOO CANDLES AND BOTTLES 53
CHAPTER 7: HOW TO MAKE MOJO BAGS 64
CHAPTER 8: THE MAGIC PRACTICES OF ROOTWORK 73
CHAPTER 9: HOODOO SPELLS TO ENHANCE YOUR LIFE 78
CHAPTER 10: LIVING A HOODOO LIFESTYLE 87
CONCLUSION 104
HERE'S ANOTHER BOOK BY SILVIA HILL THAT YOU MIGHT LIKE 105
FREE BONUS FROM SILVIA HILL AVAILABLE FOR LIMITED TIME 106
REFERENCES 107

Introduction

What does Hoodoo mean to you? Is it a religion or is it like Voodoo but sounds friendlier? Actually, Hoodoo is a unique mix of African, American, Native American, European, and Christian beliefs that have become a recognized spiritual practice that encompasses many kinds of magic and spellwork that are designed to make your life better, more successful, and give you control over what is in your future. It is based on the belief that every single item in the universe is connected, and every human, animal, place, and atom has a connection without which the world would cease to exist.

Hoodoo teaches us how to call on these connections and become part of the consciousness of the universe. It isn't a religion and won't "punish you" if you don't get it right. Hoodoo teaches us that our intentions are the fuel that powers magic. If you believe you should have something, and your intentions are pure, then the universe will work with you to ensure you get it. Everything in the natural world has a certain power, and discovering how herbs and roots bring something extra to your magic is all part of the Hoodoo experience.

Learn the magic of nature and how to create healing baths or powerful talismans for wealth and success. Begin to believe you deserve the best the universe has to offer, and you'll start to live the life you were meant to have. Rediscover your ancestors and connect to their spirits to learn from their wisdom and love. They are your personal connection to the spiritual realm and are waiting to be your guides.

Sometimes modern life means you forget the magic of nature and how your ancestors lived. The struggles they faced and the fights they had were all for your benefit. Their blood runs through your veins and gives you that ultimate connection, so use Hoodoo to benefit from this.

Chapter 1: What Is Hoodoo?

When enslaved people were transported to America between the 17th and 19th centuries for slavery purposes, they came from all areas of Africa. When they arrived on these hostile and foreign shores, all they had to unite them was their magic. The enslavers didn't approve of their African magical practices and forced them to follow Christian principles and beliefs. As generations of enslaved Black people evolved, this practice became the belief system we now know as Hoodoo.

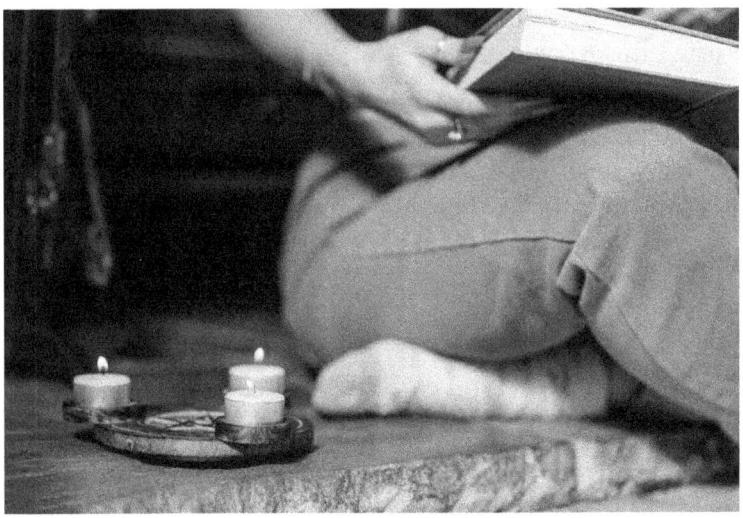

The media and other sources often mistake Hoodoo for other practices like Voodoo or Pagan beliefs.
https://www.pexels.com/photo/crop-woman-near-burning-candles-during-ritual-7256682/

The enslaved people needed to improve their lives and regain some sort of control, so they based their magic on the traditional ways each community brought with them and melded into Hoodoo. It's important to understand how African communities viewed magic and spiritualism. They didn't consider magic and connections to the spirits as a separate part of their lives. It was an intrinsic part of life that was as important as the air they breathed and when they combined these beliefs with other cultures like Native American and Central European beliefs, what emerged was a type of folk magic centered on botanical, zoological, and spiritual miasma which has developed into the modern practice we see today.

One of the more traditional beliefs of the original Hoodoo was the Kongo Cosmogram which gives a general overview of the African belief system of how the universe works and where we all come from. Humans have been creating cosmograms since the dawn of time to explain the origins of mankind, to show how the physical and spiritual realms are connected, and how the eternal circle of life explains man's existence on Earth.

Put simply, it is a reminder that everything and everybody in the physical world is connected. Without this connection, the universe would fail. It also explains the alignment to the spiritual world and how the energy created by the sun and moon at different times of the day/month and year affect us. Hoodoo rootwork and rituals can be timed using this information to gain more energy and become more effective.

These beliefs and the need for a commonality to bind the communities meant that Hoodoo became the glue the estranged enslaved people clung to. They developed spells and rituals to control their existence and began to fight back against their captors in the best way they could.

What Hoodoo Isn't

The media and other sources often mistake Hoodoo for other practices like Voodoo or Pagan beliefs. Voodoo is a religion, but Hoodoo is not. It is a spiritual practice that has deities and spirits who are worshiped, but there is no doctrine or religious significance. A lot of Hoodoo is based on Christian beliefs and the saints. Voodoo has dark magic, and although there are some Hoodoo spells to get revenge and cast curses or hexes, it isn't as dangerous as Voodoo. In Voodoo, a specific set of deities and spirits are called upon for dark magic, and it is a religion with dedicated rules and beliefs. Hoodoo is more liquid and incorporates multiple beliefs and skills.

Pagan and Wiccan beliefs have a mantra that no one will come to harm with their workings and magic, but Hoodoo has no limits regarding its magic. You can find spells and rituals to break up couples or make your boss follow your commands, but they are never meant to bring real harm to anybody, just to make their lives less comfortable.

In some parts of the US, magic performed by communities who live in the mountains is also referred to as Hoodoo because of charms, spells, and amulets. These mostly white communities have similar beliefs that all elements of nature and mankind are connected but is that Hoodoo? Some practices from the southeastern US states have been given the moniker Hill folks Hoodoo, but comparisons should be avoided if you want to get the original effect of the African-based practice.

Modern Hoodoo

By the early 1900s, Hoodoo had evolved and incorporated European and Kabalistic beliefs along with Native American and African practices, and Hoodoo root workers and conjurors were well respected in their chosen communities. They acted as doctors, magicians, and priests to those who lived there and often acted as "wise men/women."

Some practitioners took to the road with their herbal tonics, oils, and bath products. They would be a regular sight in small towns and cities peddling their magical wares. Between 1910 and 1940, many African Americans emigrated from the south to escape racism and seek employment in the more industrial north of America. This led to many receiving more formal education, which led to them abandoning their ancestral beliefs in favor of more modern faiths and structured religions.

In the mid-1990s, a Hoodoo revival began that led to the status we know today. Why should you embrace Hoodoo? Why not? Some beliefs they hold are life-changing and help you gain a more balanced view of the connection between the physical and the spiritual worlds.

Hoodoo Beliefs

- **The existence of divine providence**: Hoodoo doesn't restrict its practices to just one deity and doesn't limit who you can call on for help. Some acknowledged connections include the Buddha Hotei for prosperity and Santo Muerte for help finding a lover. Hoodoo practitioners turn to Jesus to seek protection, especially in the nighttime.

- **Life after death**: Living alongside the Divine power are the souls of those who once lived on Earth. Most rootworkers and conjurors work with ancestors and the spirits of the dead to make their magic work. When you die, you don't cease to exist. You simply ascend to a higher realm where you are dedicated to assisting the living. Ancestors and the spirits of the dead regularly commune with the divine on our behalf.

- **Divination**: Hoodoo work is often based on what will happen in the future. These events are told to us by the ancestors using divination tools like bones and paying cards. This allows humans to change the course of their futures to shift probabilities and create a more successful outcome.

- **Retributive justice**: Unlike other spiritual practices that teach us to "do no harm" whatever the circumstances, Hoodoo works on the principle from Biblical times that states "an eye for an eye," which allows the person who has been wronged to retaliate. However, the retribution must fit the crime, or there will be recriminations.

- **Intention**: Hoodoo teaches us that intentions are the keys to life. Even if you use a hexing powder, it will only affect someone who deserves the curse. Anyone else who encounters the powder will be unaffected. Curses and wishes only work when a higher being approves them. Pure intentions are the fuel of Hoodoo magic.

In summary, Hoodoo originated in America brought by enslaved Africans who had been stripped of their belongings, identities, and religion. They had been ripped from their homelands and subjected to cruelty and degradation that many of us cannot even imagine. Working together to keep their traditional beliefs and practices alive, they combined their arts with the Christian religion they were forced to adopt and developed the magical practice called Hoodoo.

Your Hoodoo experience will be unique to you. Because it is based on your energy, intentions, and connections to the universe, everybody will react differently to the spells and rituals they perform. That is the beauty of Hoodoo. It is whatever you need it to be, and provided you have clear intentions and come from a good place, you'll be heard. You will succeed, and you will become part of the Hoodoo community.

Chapter 2: Hoodoo Deities and Spirits

Hoodoo is the most eclectic form of magic today, and when the enslaved people that formed the practice came together from all the different areas of the African continent, they had to find a way to communicate. They spoke different languages and followed different religions, but they were ultimately under the control of American enslavers who only allowed them to practice Catholicism. Due to this mishmash of their original African roots and Christianity, Hoodoo evolved into a magic practice that embraced many deities and spirits from a multitude of cultures.

St. Joseph of Cupertino.
https://commons.wikimedia.org/wiki/File:SaintJosephCupertino.jpg

The practice has been evolving and growing for over four hundred years and has embraced religions and deities from across the globe. Today people who practice Hoodoo focus on the Christian - Jewish roots combined with the traditional African spirits known as the Lao to escape the traditional confines of modern Christianity. They recognize that in the past, they were maligned by white supremacy by the church and stripped of their self-esteem when their traditional beliefs and communication methods were deemed as evil and devil worshipping.

The enslavers of the day were determined to drive any African traditions and beliefs underground, but the slaves knew they needed that connection with their ancestors and their magic connection to nature. The spells and rituals they used were conjured to help them take a measure of control over their lives and improve their lot as enslaved people. They also used their belief in God to make them feel stronger and identify his presence in all of nature.

What Is a Conjurer?

Understanding how Hoodoo works starts with the conjurer. They represented the knowledge and wisdom of the earth and nature and how to connect the physical world with the spiritual realm by using natural substances like herbs and roots combined with magical practices to connect to deities and spirits. As the African beliefs assimilated into the Christian religious base, Germanic and European influences were added to them. The US was a mixing pot of cultures, and, as a result, Hoodoo became a melded tradition of conjure that exists today.

Conjure has two main streams: the practice and wisdom passed down by conjure-orientated families who rely on their ancestors for advice and power. The second stream relies on more formal education sources. These conjurers use religious and scientific texts from other religions to learn and improve their magic practices. Conjure doctors would seek out respected grimoires and other religious texts about the occult to incorporate them into their own Hoodoo traditions.

It is believed that if anybody showed a natural gift for these beliefs, they would be taught by their peers how to become a conjurer. They would be taught traditional and more contemporary ways to connect with the spirits and their ancestors to commune with them and learn from their wisdom. Herbs and plants were known to have certain powers, and conjurers would work with them along with natural elements to control the flow of energies and improve the situations of the people that consulted them.

Today we can use the same principles to tap into the power of nature and change our lives. It isn't dangerous or even disrespectful to the church. Hoodoo isn't religious. It is simply magical and focuses on connecting to the natural world for effective results and the power to manifest results.

The Importance of God and the Saints in Hoodoo

Hoodoo is not a religion but is intrinsically entwined with Christianity, especially Protestant Christianity. Conjurers would use a practice called "Pleading the Blood" to add the power of the resurrection of Jesus to their spells. The power of life over death and the resurrection of Jesus brought the ultimate power of Christ that could be applied to any spell by using the phrase "I plead the blood of Jesus..." to power their work.

Hoodoo believes that the Bible is the ultimate spell/magic book and that Moses was the most acclaimed conjurer of all time. They don't believe in the Christian "You will obey or be damned" variety of the religion. Most Christians read the Bible and try to live by the commandments, while Hoodoo practitioners embrace the biblical God and his son, Jesus, the Holy Trinity, and the prophets and saints. They believe that Christianity gives them the power to fight demons, raise the dead, repel poisoners and be impervious to the devil. If you read the Bible as it was meant to be read, you'll realize that Hoodoo practices are much truer to the text than traditional Christian practices.

The Bible and Christianity were used for generations to justify slavery and the atrocities carried out by white enslavers in the past, but if you study the work of conjurors, you'll find they are closer to the true beliefs of Christianity than regular churchgoers. Hoodoo folk believe they have a connection to God and that he calls them to do his work on Earth, while most churchgoers believe the opposite and are content to worship past glories and have zero spiritual connections.

Working with the saints merely involves choosing the Christian saint <u>who</u> represents the power you need to fuel your root work. Most people know the more celebrated saints, but there are hundreds, if not thousands, of saints you can call upon to connect to you. There are Coptic saints, Russian, Irish, Jesuit, venerable, and blessed saints to choose from, so do your research and start connecting to the higher energies they bring.

Here are a few suggestions for some lesser-known saints who had incredible powers

1. **St Joseph of Cupertino, a.k.a. the flying saint.** This levitating saint didn't just fly in front of a couple of people once. He regularly flew into the sky in front of large groups of people, and once, he even levitated during an audience with the pope. It was reported that even mentioning God or one of the saints would send this maverick saint into the air. His constant flying soon became a problem, and the church labeled him a disruptive influence and locked him in a cell for the rest of his life.

2. **St. Catherine of Alexandria** was the ultimate conversion machine. Born a princess in Egypt in the 3rd century, she was well-educated and practiced paganism until she reached her teens. She claimed to have been visited by the Virgin Mary, who told Catherine that she was married to Christ in a spiritual union and that she should embrace the Christian faith. Catherine was so affected by the vision that she converted immediately. The Emperor of Rome at the time held an audience with her when she tried to persuade him to stop persecuting Christians, and despite his best efforts, she managed to convert some members of his court. The emperor was furious and imprisoned her, but she continued to convert the prisoners. He then tried to persuade her to stop by proposing marriage to her. When she refused, he sentenced her to death by the spiked wheel, but when the instrument shattered, he ordered her to be beheaded instead. She was finally executed with an ax.

3. **St. Vincent Ferrer** was raising the dead. Vincent was a theologian praised for his missionary work, but his most spectacular feat was bringing someone back from the dead. He was attending a procession leading a man to his death for his part in a crime that Vincent knew was unjust, and the man was innocent. He tried to plead with the officials responsible for the execution, but his pleas fell on deaf ears. At the same time, a corpse was being carried through the streets on a stretcher, and Vincent asked the corpse, "Is this man guilty?" the corpse sat up and answered, "No, he is not," before he lay back down on the stretcher. Vincent asked the dead man if he required a reward for his intervention, and the man replied, "No, for I am assured of salvation" before he promptly died again.

High John the Conqueror

Another powerful influence in Hoodoo culture is High John, a mighty tall man transported across the sea from Africa to serve as an enslaved person. He was a clever wily man who loved to avoid work and trick his master with his intelligence. If he had a shovel in the field, it would break, if he went to the shed, it would burn down, but his real skills were getting one over on his "Massa."

When John's master would be ready to whip him, John would turn around and work earnestly, exceeding any other worker in the field, and his master would calm his temper and let him live another day. He was also a master fisherman, and his master accompanied him to the fishing hole to help improve his skills. John admired the walking stick his master was carrying and said, "That's the finest three-ended stick I have ever seen," to which the master replied, "John, this stick has only two ends, and I bet you a chicken that you can't prove otherwise."

John replied, "No, it has three ends, this end is the handle, and the silver pointy end is the second one." He then took the walking stick to the swimming hole and threw it in. "See, Massa, that's the third end of your stick." His master realized he had been outwitted and paid John his chicken.

Another popular story revolved around John being tasked to prepare the turkey ready for Christmas. His master told him that whatever he did to the turkey, he would do to John. If John cut the turkey's head off, his head would be removed, and if he plucked the bird, the master would probably skin John alive.

On Christmas morning, the family was waiting for their turkey to arrive and expecting a good laugh at poor John's fate. He arrived with the turkey following behind him, attached to a red string. John approached the porch and greeted his master. He then picked the turkey up, turned it around, and kissed it on the butt. The master turned purple because he was so annoyed, and as he blustered and his eyes bulged, John turned around slowly, raised his butt slightly, and said, "Take your time; I got all day, folks!"

Enslaved people had very little to laugh about, and you can imagine them huddled in groups telling the tales of High John and his antics before belly-laughing at the foolish master and how John had tricked him.

Connect to Your Ancestors

Most spiritual and magic workers know the importance of connections with the past and how generations living before us can influence their work. Your ancestors determine your DNA. They lived their lives at different times, yet when you express emotions, you are connecting to their spirits. They lived through hard times so you could benefit from their toil, and they learned lessons so they could pass on their knowledge.

Modern religions have steered us away from ancestral ties, which means we sometimes forget where we come from. The blood that runs through your veins is a direct result of your ancestors, and the worship of their power remains part of a cultural pattern in various areas of the world like India, Asia, China, and among the Native Indians. Let's take time to celebrate these connections and remember our roots.

Different Ways to Connect to Your Ancestors
Genealogy
You can use multiple resources to trace your family tree, and even though it may seem daunting, it can be tremendous fun. There are multiple archives online and advice on how to start tracing your roots back to your ancestors. The first couple of generations, including your

parents and grandparents, can prove to be an effective way to bring your family closer and discover what they lived through and how their childhoods differed from yours.

DNA Analysis

This relatively new technology allows you to delve back in time and discover your ancestors' origins. You could find ties to the Vikings, Celts, or even medieval ancestors. You just don't know what you'll discover and the advantages it will give you in your magic.

Scrapbooking

Once you have details of your ancestors and their occupations and places where they lived, you can start to build a comprehensive scrapbook of your findings. Create a sacred book that can be designated to their memories, and make a page for each of your ancestors. Use the tree of life design to create a spiritual family tree and enter anything relevant and interesting to strengthen your connection.

Create a Section on Your Altar for Your Ancestors

We will cover this in the chapter dedicated to altar and shrine creation later in the book.

Invite Them into Your Dreams

Ask them to come, and your ancestors will visit you in your dreams. They may be relatives you already know about, but they could be ancestors that haven't yet been discovered. Ask pertinent questions, and you will get the answers you need. They will then be with you in spirit whenever you need them and will bring strength and wisdom to your Hoodoo work and other sections of your life. Remember to keep a notebook by your bedside table to record your dreams as part of your normal routine.

Pray to Your Ancestors

Regardless of your religious beliefs, the power of prayer cannot be overlooked. Prayer is another way to show respect and connect to your higher beings and energies. You don't have to kneel or bow your head. You must just be respectful and sincere. Talk to them as if they were in the room with you and listen to every word you say. Do it in your head or speak out loud, depending on what makes you feel more comfortable and enjoy the experience. They are just as overjoyed to hear your voice as you should be to form these connections.

Recreate Crafts They Would Have Enjoyed

Ancient skills have been forgotten, and the only place you see modern people making their own fires and hunting food is on the television in survival programs. Learning how to do these elemental skills will make you more adept at survival and keeps the connection to your more distant ancestors alive. You can still follow your more recent ancestors' skills by taking up crochet or knitting if it was something your grandmother did. Was your grandfather a skilled hunter or fisherman? Take up the hobby they loved doing and feel those connections strengthen. Ask family members if they have original tools from your heritage that you can use. A pair of knitting needles or a fishing rod that is unfused with their energy will help your connection become more personal.

Foods and Drinks

Celebrate your heritage at the dinner table by recreating dishes that originate from your ancestral ties. Is your family Irish? Soda bread is so simple to make, and Irish stew is a fabulous family meal you can share with a table full of people. Serve a side of colcannon with tasty potatoes and spring onions accompanied by a pint of Guinness and toast your Celtic relatives. Are your family from the West Indies? Make spicy curries and soul food to celebrate their heritage. Food and drink are the staples of life, and forming connections can be exciting as well as being a new experience for your taste buds.

Rituals and Meditation

Some people are skilled at creating rituals to connect to their ancestors, but sometimes beginners need more detailed instructions. Follow the ritual below to connect to your ancestors and safely cross the veil between this world and theirs.

What You Need

- Four white candles
- One red tea light
- Five holders for your candles
- Olive oil to dress your candles
- Protective herbs to keep you safe (basil, cumin, or clover will work but choose your own depending on your preferences)

- An herb with links to your ancestor's homeland (get creative here and research the herbs that are popular in Italy, for instance, or Eastern Germany)
- A dish for rolling. You can also use a cutting board as a candle rolling area
- Red ribbon or string
- Lighter or matches
- Incense to bring strength to your work (dragons blood works well)
- Incense to commemorate your ancestor's homeland
- Divination tools for your ancestors to speak through, cards or dice, bones or runes, whatever tools you are familiar with

Choose a time when the veil between the two worlds is at its flimsiest, like dusk or midnight. Choose a lunar phase incorporating the Dark of the Full moon to bring strength to your work.

Prepare the area for your ritual by cleansing it with sage or another method of smudging or sweeping. Now take a bath to make sure you are free from negative energies. Take all your supplies into the center of the room and decide where your sacred circle will be. Set the four white candles in the corners to indicate the four points of the circle, north, east, south, and west. Make sure you have plenty of room to work in and gather the remaining supplies in your work area.

Cast the Circle

1. Position yourself at the northern point of the area and take the lighter in your hand. Imagine yourself in a vast cave filled with white light reflecting off walls filled with crystals.
2. Call upon the element of the north, which is the earth, by raising your arms and saying, "I call on you to nourish me and protect me from all evil on this magical night." Light the white candle of the north.
3. Now turn to the west of the circle and ask for the element of water to assist you before you light the candle.
4. Repeat the exercise in the following two corners invoking the elements of fire and air before lighting the candles to complete your circle.

5. Now state, "The circle is now cast, and let no spirit or energy enter this sacred space without my direct invitation."

Your circle is now cast and ready for your ritual. If you have a preferred method of casting a circle, ignore the instructions above and use your method instead.

Call Your Ancestors
1. Put the oil and chosen herbs on your anointing dish or board and roll the red candle in the liquid.
2. As you roll the candle, imagine your ancestors watching over you and how they look. Remember the struggles they endured in their lifetimes and the joys they felt when they succeeded. Imagine how they feel connecting to you at that moment as you dress your candle.
3. Place the candle in the holder and light your intensifying incense.
4. Raise the energy in the circle by doing your favorite activity. Dance, chant, or pray to increase the energy and positivity in the circle, and take as long as you like.
5. Once you feel the levels are at their optimum, light the red candle.
6. Take the red string or yarn, weave it through your fingers, hold your hands to your heart, and say the following words: "*I call upon my ancestors to join me in this world. I lead the way with this symbolic light and ask those who have gone before me to protect me in this dimension. Bring your strength and wisdom to my world, and I invite only the ancestors that have my best wishes in their hearts. I thank them for the blood, sweat, and tears they shed for me to allow me to enjoy my life on this earth.*"
7. Ensure the string or yarn is secure and not a fire hazard by tying it securely around your wrist.
8. Light the offertory incense and say, "*May my offering of scented smoke bring you joy and cement our relationship. I give you this offering to celebrate the protection and love you bring to my world. So it shall be.*"

9. Now sit and speak to the relatives you have summoned. You may wish to use your divination tools to assist the conversation or use your psychic abilities to hear them. Listen to what they are saying and let the session last for as long as the candle takes to burn down.
10. Once the ritual has ended, thank the ancestors for their input and the messages they have sent you.
11. Close the circle by snuffing out the candles, releasing the elements in turn, and thanking them for their assistance.

Once the ritual is complete, it's time to ground yourself and recover from the excess energy you created. A simple meal of bread and cheese with a soothing cup of tea will help, or you can meditate to regain your equilibrium. Moving on will take a couple of hours, and this is normal, so don't worry. Once your energy levels have been restored to normal, you can sleep and recover.

The ritual remains will include the incense ashes and the candles' wax. Take a red bag, place these remains in the bag, and tie it with the red string. Hang it on your door for protection, or carry it with you so you can feel their protection throughout the day. Use the bag to center yourself if you require further communication with your relatives.

Remember that you have formed a contract with your ancestors, and this should be celebrated with regular offerings. Leave a glass of wine on your shrine or even a simple cup of coffee every week. Place an item of food or a small bunch of flowers. Your offerings should reflect their personality and what they enjoyed on Earth before they passed.

Loa Spirits

A more traditional form of spirit in Hoodoo centers upon the Loa spirits, an original form of spirit from the Voodoo tradition that Hoodoo has adapted to bring benevolence and love to the magic. They are connected to the voodoo dolls and headless chickens in the movies, but the Loa are important spirits that you can choose to work with or ignore.

They are the Hoodoo version of guardian angels who guard the realms of the dead, and while figures like Papa Legba or Baron Samedi may seem dangerous and frightening, some Hoodoo practitioners will call on them when they need added power to fight their enemies. This is not something beginners should try, and even advanced Hoodoo rootworkers would stay away from the Loa. They are mentioned here purely as a source of reference and a matter of interest. They inspired the Hoodoo's use of poppets and mojo bags for added magic.

Chapter 3: Ingredients and Materials You Need

Original Hoodoo practitioners had little to choose from to form their spells and potions. They were enslaved and didn't have access to materials apart from what was in their environment. As enslaved people, they would be responsible for food preparation and would often have a full run of the kitchen. This explains why a lot of their spells and magic are based on the power of herbs and roots. As the enslaved people converged in the US, they brought their knowledge of magical herbs and roots with them and worked together to make their Hoodoo magic stronger and more effective.

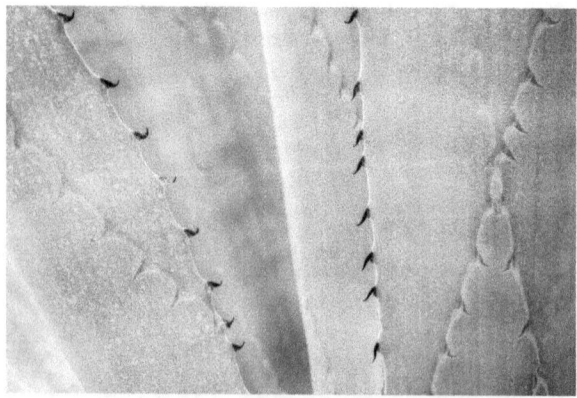

Used for protection and security, aloe vera plants would often be planted at the doorways of the home to keep evil spirits away.
https://www.pexels.com/photo/close-up-photography-of-aloe-vera-plant-1578504/

Magical Hoodoo Herbs and Roots

Adam and Eve Root, also known as the putty root or Aplectrum

This root was used to promote relationships and help couples form stronger bonds. It was a popular ingredient in potions to cure sexual problems and promote fertility and sexual energy. The root originated from an orchid found in eastern parts of the US and Canada, and the leaves are pinstripe with dark green stripes. The male part of the plant was carried by the man, while the woman carried the female part to ensure they would stay together and remain faithful. A new love was also attracted to practitioners who carried the Adam and Eve root in their mojo bags.

Unfortunately, the plant is now labeled as endangered, and products purported to contain the root will probably have a substitute ingredient. Make sure any products you buy have sourced their ingredients ethically.

Allspice Berries

Original Hoodoo workers used these to bring good luck and prosperity. Gamblers would take allspice berries when they played games of chance or needed luck in business matters. Today the allspice berries are known for relieving psychological stress and anxiety. Allspice is also known as Jamaican pepper, myrtle, and pimento and can be found in all good spice shops. If you want to prepare your own, pick the berries of the Pimenta tree and dry them in the sun.

Alfalfa

Also called lucerne, this plant is cultivated for foraging, used as food for livestock and cattle, and made into hay for the winter. It has recently emerged as a superfood because it is packed with vitamins and is effective in boosting your immune system. Hoodoo uses rootwork for general good luck, money spells, and overall prosperity. Keep it in your purse or in a money box to attract money to you and your family.

Alkanet Root

This herb from the borage family was used to dye clothes red and was a common part of Hoodoo work. It attracts money and increases good luck.

Aloe Vera

Used for protection and security, aloe vera plants would often be planted at the doorways of the home to keep evil spirits away. Today the plant is widely available and provides a decorative plant for the home.

Angelica Root

Also known as the Holy Ghost or Archangel root, this herb is a form of wild celery that has impressive health benefits. It is a staple ingredient in Hoodoo workings and should be included in potions to help women find strength and peace. It also breaks jinxes and is a powerful guardian for the user. Carry this in your mojo bag to ward off evil spirits and attract luck and prosperity.

Anise

Also called aniseed, this potent plant is a powerful protection ingredient that keeps evil spirits at bay and helps the rootworker to enhance their psychic abilities. Some Hoodoo spells include anise to connect with the spirits.

Basil

Widely used in the kitchen in Hoodoo, this common herb brings love and happiness to a household and is representative of peace and harmony. It is associated with the Haitian goddess Erzulie and the Hindu god Vishnu.

Bay Leaves

A common ingredient, bay leaves are incredibly powerful in Hoodoo spells. They bring protection, security, and clarity of mind to spells. They also ward off evil spirits and banish enemies, ensuring victory in conflicts. Use them in potions for increased health and spirituality and to increase personal insight.

Black Peppercorns

Whole black peppercorns were added to spells to enable revenge for the spell caster and to cause pain and sorrow to their enemies. Use them to guard your home against unwanted visitors and evil spirits.

Buckeye Nuts

In the UK, these nuts are called conkers and are used in childhood games, but when used in the US, they are a potent ingredient in Hoodoo practices. They bring power and luck and increase sexual potency for users.

Cactus

Use the spines to jinx your enemies or as protection from evil and attacks.

Catnip

A plant from the mint family, which has a pungent smell that attracts cats, is also a powerful way to attract women. Men should carry it in their pockets to attract the fairer sex and increase their sexual potency.

Cayenne Pepper

This popular ingredient in spicy Cajun dishes is also used to create chaos in your enemies' households and drive away your enemies.

Chamomile

A fragrant herb popular in teas, chamomile is a general good luck ingredient and will help you calm your household and remove any financial jinxes.

Clover

A popular plant in folklore from diverse cultures, this is a commonly used ingredient for good luck and prosperity. It is also used to promote love and fidelity in relationships. Its leaves are thought to represent the holy trinity, and three leaves are more sacred than four.

Coconut

Use the whole coconut to represent the whole head and the mind. You can work with the coconut to dominate the target's thoughts and experiences to reward or punish them depending on your intentions.

Dandelion

This common weed is a potent ingredient for granting wishes and increasing psychic visions.

Devil's Dung

This aromatic and pungent dried latex originates from the roots of the rhizome root and is used to repel illness and evil. Also known as asafetida, it is named after the Latin term "foetidus" which literally means stinky. Use it to protect your home and family from evil and cast curses on those who would harm you. Wear gloves while you work, as the smell will linger for days on your bare skin.

Devils' Shoestring

This member of the pea family will often appear on the dining table and is a powerful herb in most witchcraft. The long stringy stems are thought to be effective in tripping the devil and keeping him away from your house. Carry the roots when gambling, and luck will follow you.

Dill

Another popular herb found in most kitchens, dill is added to spells and potions to break love curses and lift any jinxes placed on the practitioner. It brings luck in legal matters and reinforces sexual feelings and attraction.

Dragon's Blood

A natural plant resin that originates from the sedum plant dragon's blood is used in spells for protection and general good luck. Use in potions to bring prosperity and luck when gambling.

Fennel

Wild fennel is a hardy plant that is delicious in recipes, but in Hoodoo, it represents a barrier against legal issues and keeps away meddlers who want to know your business. Use it in spells to protect your home from troublesome spirits.

Five Finger Grass

Also known as cinquefoil, this plant looks like a human hand with its five segmented leaves. It is used to draw money and wealth and improve career prospects. Carry it with you when you travel to keep you and your money safe from harm. Five-finger grass is also a powerful plant for uncrossing curses and hexes.

Garlic

Popular in vampire lore, garlic is the ultimate protection ingredient.

Ginger

A fiery spicy ingredient in food, it also brings heat to Hoodoo spells. Use it to inflame passions and bring luck to gamblers.

Ginseng

Traditionally used in sex potions, Hoodoo practitioners used ginseng to protect themselves and their loved ones.

High John the Conqueror

One of the staple ingredients in any Hoodoo household, the root is obtained from the plant Ipomoea purga and is used for prosperity, luck, and the strength to conquer your enemies. See chapter 2 for more details about John and his origins.

Holly

The popular leafy green plant protects the home by placing it at the doorway and in windows.

Ivy

Another popular and fast-growing plant you should use is ivy to keep your home safe.

Jasmine

Use this pleasantly scented herb to bring love and joy to your potions and spells.

Job's Tears

A tall growing grass crop, the roots and the seeds are both used in Hoodoo root work. They represent the wishes of the worker and ensure they come true. The seeds should be carried when gambling to bring success and good luck.

Juniper

The lush green leaves and roots of this tree bring love and luck to your work, and the berries are used to create teas and baths to increase sexual attraction.

Lemon Balm

Use in baths and potions to cleanse the body and soul while dispelling any bad luck regarding your relationships. It draws in new love and attracts healthy connections.

Lettuce

Any kind of lettuce will do. Use the leaves to draw money towards you. The fresh leaves on the darker types of lettuce work best.

Licorice Root

Used to command the will of others and make them bend to your will. Use it to dominate and control your enemies.

Lucky Hand Root

This root is from a wild orchid named the salep and is a highly regarded ingredient in magical terms. It gives extraordinarily strong protection and luck, especially in gambling.

Magnolia Leaves

The leaves from the flowering magnolia should be used to control husbands with wandering eyes. Keep them faithful and focused on their wives with this ingredient.

Mandrake Root

Originally from the nightshade family of plants, this root has regained notoriety due to its use in popular Harry Potter stories. Carve the root into a doll form to inspire love and passion, or carry it in its original form to bring prosperity.

Mimosa

You may know it as a tasty cocktail, but in magic, the mimosa genus contains over five hundred species of plants. The leaves of the common mimosa tree are used for protection in spells and potions.

Mint

Common wild mint brings fresh and cooling energy to your spells. It can calm arguments and bring peace to your home. Use it to create barriers your enemies cannot cross and keep yourself safe. Carry it with you to increase your psychic abilities.

Mistletoe

A common parasite in the natural world, mistletoe is used to ward off all forms of evil. Hang it in your thresholds to protect yourself from evil and keep your home safe.

Mustard Seed

Use this common ingredient to improve male sexual energy and restore luck, especially in business.

Nutmeg

Another common kitchen ingredient, you can use nutmeg to attract love and bring good luck.

Orris Root

Also known as the Queen Elizabeth root, it is originally sourced from the rootstock of the iris flower. It tastes like raspberry and is used to flavor tinctures and potions. In Hoodoo, it is used to attract men to women and is also used by men to control their enemies.

Onion
The common onion is often used for protection, and its pungent odor both cleanses and repels evil.

Parsley
The common herb found in most kitchens has specific powers in Hoodoo. Use it when negotiating housing issues like rental or negotiating contracts to ensure success. Parsley is used to celebrate the passing of relatives and loved ones and to increase fertility.

Patchouli
A strong-smelling oil patchouli is used to draw love and money to the wearer and uncross any hexes placed on them.

Raspberry Leaves
Use it to create fidelity in your relationship and bring good luck to you both.

Rose
This fragrant flower is used to bring luck and love to your household.

Rosemary
Especially powerful for spells cast for and by women. It brings good dreams and keeps them safe and empowered. Use rosemary to bring strength and femininity to your work.

Rue
A sprig of this evergreen bush worn under your clothes will ward off evil and make you impervious to the evil eye.

Sage
A protective and potent herb for cleansing your home and bringing blessings to your door. It is especially powerful for female users and attracts wisdom and knowledge to the user.

Spanish Moss
This moss is often found growing on trees in subtropical climates, but it can be bought from good herbal outlets. Use dried Spanish moss to stuff your poppets or dolls used in your Hoodoo practices. It can be used to jinx and curse others or draw money to your spells.

Thyme

Add thyme to your spells to stop bad dreams and bring peace of mind. It also has strong financial benefits.

Violet

Use the violet's flowers and roots when dealing with innocence and chastity. It brings pure and innocent power to your spells and can be used in potions or in baths.

Willow

The magnificent willow tree is a powerful part of Hoodoo magic; the leaves are used for protection and health. Use it to attract love and passion.

Witch Grass

Also known as devil's grass, this common ingredient is used to break up lovers and cast spells on your enemies. When dried, it can be used to stuff dolls and poppets.

Yarrow

Also known as old man's pepper and the devil's nettle, yarrow is a perennial herb that is found in the wild. It is used for courage and to make the user brave in times of conflict. It is also used for divination purposes.

Tools for Conjure

Just like the herbs and plants they used, Hoodoo workers were restricted by their lack of possessions and had to make do with their everyday tools. This means that conjuring tools are often multipurpose items found in the house or nature. No fancy implements or exotic items need to be cleansed at certain times of the day or kept sacred. Hoodoo is all about everyday folk using everyday items to create magic.

Today, Hoodoo tools can be more ornate and purchased from dedicated sites and stores, but keeping your magic real should involve using tools that resemble the original Hoodoo practitioners used.

Below are some ordinary items that can be used for magic – and an explanation of how they can provide multiple uses, keeping it simple and inexpensive to practice the craft.

Screwdriver

Every household should have a screwdriver, and, in magic, these handy tools are perfect for writing on your wax candles and carving symbols on pliable materials. Use it to make holes to insert oils and herbs into your candles to make them more potent and magical.

Wine Glasses

Flat-based glasses can obviously be used to hold wine, but they can also be used to cover open flames when they are burning down to form seals.

Aluminum Cans

Perhaps the most versatile items in your home. Wash them out and use them to hold candles, melt the wax to form your own candle, or deposit burning pieces of paper with spells and petitions on them so they can burn safely. Use the cans to keep your herbs and roots in, and engrave the lids with a list of what they contain. Use tuna cans for more shallow burning needs or substitute with metal ashtrays instead.

Laces and Ribbons from Old Clothes or Shoes

Use these to perform cord magic and add color and texture to your spells.

Saucers

Because of the curved shape of the common saucer, you can place pieces of paper with your spells under the saucer and then burn a candle on the surface. They are sturdy enough for pillar candles to sit on and are handy to store.

Coin Purses

Later in this book, we will cover the art of making mojo bags, but if you haven't had time to make one, then a coin purse will do for now.

Cork Coasters

These handy objects are the perfect size for use as talismans, and you can easily burn magical symbols on the cork for an effective appearance.

Cutting Board

Because they are designed for mixing ingredients and working with food, they are perfect as candle boards. Use a cutting board to spread herbs and powders into a mixture in which you can roll your oil-anointed candles to ensure a smooth and complete coverage.

Children's Dolls

If you enjoy the idea of a poppet or a Hoodoo doll but don't have the time to make your own, any action figure or child's doll will work. Choose one for housing your spirits or to represent an individual.

Board Game Tokens

The tokens used in Monopoly and Cluedo are great for representing your needs and desires in mojo bags. The shoe represents travel, the money sack is financial strength, and the rope is a binding tool. Search for other tokens in more abstract places to make your collection quirky and magical. Tokens from arcades are also a decorative way to improve your magic tool arsenal and depict all forms of magical images. Look out for them on Internet auction sites and in antique shops.

Candles

One of the staple parts of your tool collection, you should have candles of varying colors and sizes so you can adapt them to your needs. Candles are everywhere, and there is no need to splash too much cash when buying your candles, especially when you are a beginner.

Divining Items

Some Hoodoo practitioners have a psychic connection with the spirits and use traditional divination methods to connect to them and foresee the future. Most readings are from items thrown by the user onto a clean white cloth and interpreted by traditional methods to predict the future. These items can be as diverse as dried bones. Chicken bones are perfect when dried or use stones or crystals.

Playing cards are another cheap and effortless way to practice divination, and an ordinary pack can be used for beginners. When you decide that cards are your preferred method of connecting with the spirits, you can progress onto specially designed Hoodoo cards that are both decorative and more dedicated to the magical world.

Dice are popular divination tools and can be read simply using instructions. They also represent a connection to the olden ways as they were often made from bones, so if the thought of handling actual bones repels you, try to find a set of dice made from bone instead.

Paper for writing petitions to the spirits

Brown grocery sacks are hardy and handy for writing your petitions, but the paper you choose isn't that important. What you write on it is the key to conjuring the response you require.

Some practitioners have adapted tools from other practices, but the original Hoodoo rootworkers didn't have that luxury. Keep costs low and be creative with your spiritual toolbox.

Dust and Dirt in Hoodoo

You will have noticed that there are no bowls or mixing implements here; they will be covered in the chapter about your Hoodoo altar. Also, many spells and traditional Hoodoo practices used dirt, more specifically graveyard dirt, which is now considered inappropriate and, in most cases, illegal. The thought of somebody entering a graveyard and taking the soil from a grave doesn't sit well in today's society, so it's probably best if you don't use it.

Alternative sources come from burning coffee grounds, patchouli leaves, sage, or other flammable sources that can be burned safely. Another alternative is to burn any plants from your garden that have withered and died to represent the connection to the dead, but as most Hoodoo practices are concentrated on connecting to your ancestors, this may seem redundant. However, if you believe that the spirits of the dead plant are just as powerful as human spirits, this gives you a safe way to connect to the afterlife. As with all your magic work, the choice is yours.

You may still want to practice the original art by using dust or dirt from crossroads. This represents turning a corner and is used in spells where a decision needs to be made, or a change in circumstances is required. Collect dirt from a place that is a recognized crossroad or a place that represents your personal space, depending on the spells you are conducting. There are no fixed rules, as crossroads mean different things to different people.

Keeping a Checklist of Your Tools and Ingredients

Who said that witches and root workers couldn't be organized? Just like you have a shopping list for your kitchen, it can be helpful to keep a checklist for your Hoodoo work. Keep a list of your favorite herbs and ingredients somewhere you can check them regularly and refill any of your ingredients that are getting low.

Chapter 4: Getting Ready for Hoodoo

How do you prepare for a job interview? What do you do before a big date? What rituals do you follow in the morning to ensure you face the day at your best? You prepare using certain routines, take extra care over your appearance, and take care of any items you need to use to make these experiences better and more successful. So why are you wondering what to do before starting your Hoodoo practice? Inexperience in beginners sometimes mean they forget the basic rules of life regarding Hoodoo. They are so committed to getting to the fun stuff that they forget that the prep is just as important as the process, if not more.

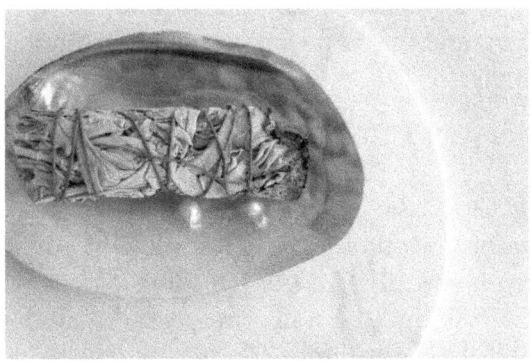

Cleansing with smoke helps you breathe in the healing smoke and let go of the negativity and excess anxiety.
https://www.pexels.com/photo/a-burning-sage-on-a-shell-with-pearls-6766465/

First, let's answer some FAQs about cleansing and why it's so important

1. **Why is spiritual cleansing so important?**

Negative energy will accumulate in your energy field during normal life. You are regularly subject to stress, anger, fear, and other negative forces and absorb negativity from other people in your space. Removing this energy will clear your spiritual aura and allow positivity to flow to you. Your sacred space is also subject to these negative forces; some spirits and divine beings will be more likely to visit clean and positive spaces. After all, who wants to visit somewhere filled with negativity and spiritual debris?

2. **Why should we clean our sacred spaces even if nobody has been there?**

If your sacred space is in your home or your garden, it will be affected by your visitors, even if they are nearby and not in the actual space. All the traffic that flows through your home and the energies they carry will invade your space even through airborne means. Remember that you also carry your own negative forces into the space and deposit them whenever possible. It isn't worth the risk of muddying your energies with negativity just to avoid a cleansing beforehand.

3. **What rituals should I use?**

As with all cleansing rituals, you tend to follow a set pattern and use materials that suit your needs. Spiritual cleansing is just the same. We will consider some effective cleansing methods that you can try and choose the ones that feel right for you. In time the methods you use will become so natural that you won't even think about them, and they will come naturally.

Self-Cleansing Rituals

- **Bathing.** A classic relaxing bath in water infused with salts, herbs, roots, or other ingredients will help you relax physically and metaphorically. Add crystals and play soothing music to help you sink into the water and let go of all that negativity. If you don't have a bathtub, consider bathing in a natural water source. Taking a dip in the ocean or a cool flowing stream will cleanse and recharge your spirit and leave you connected to

nature.
- **Smudging.** Cleansing with smoke helps you breathe in the healing smoke and let go of the negativity and excess anxiety. Use classic sage to cleanse yourself, or choose from the multiple cleansing herbs that will do the job just as well. Try rosemary, rose, lavender, or citrus leaves to mix it up a bit. Mix your herbs and light them safely to smudge your aura, and move the smudging stick from your head to your toes in a sweeping motion to clear your body and mind.
- **Crystal cleansing.** Crystals provide a powerful way to draw negative energy from you. Use selenite or black tourmaline to remove the energy from your personal space by passing them over your body to absorb the destructive energy forces.
- **Fire cleansing.** Older forms of Hoodoo used the element fire to cleanse people who had been possessed and filled with the spirit of another, but today we can use the same principle to cleanse our bodies and minds. Jumping over a bonfire was a ritual that has been consigned to history because of safety issues, but you can still represent the element with an unlit candle. Choose a white candle and then roll it over your body to absorb the harmful energy by lighting it once the ritual has been fulfilled.
- **Magical sprays.** Spraying yourself with liquid infused with magical properties is a great alternative to bathing. If you don't have time for a shower or bath, then use a cleansing spray to bring positivity to your body and feel refreshed and ready to work your magic.
- **Detox.** Using healing teas and other detox liquids will cleanse you from within and help you feel refreshed and hydrated.
- **Egg cleansing.** If you love thinking outside the box, try this nifty way to cleanse using nature's products. Take an egg in its shell and roll it over your body. Make sure you cover the entire body and even roll it over your face and head. Now crack the egg in a bowl of water and see what it tells you. If the yolk is dull or the white is cloudy, it is a clear sign that you have transferred your negative energies into the egg.

- **Cleanse your energy directly.** Use ancient methods like Reiki or yoga to boost your positivity and banish the residual energy lurking there. We will examine meditations you can also use later in this chapter.

Cleansing Rituals for Your Home

- **Smoke cleansing.** Smudging for the home is just as effective as it is for the body. Use traditional herbs and rid your sacred space of negative energy. Make sure you are safe and have methods for always dowsing the fire and smoke. Remember to open the windows to allow the harmful energies to escape and clear the smoke. You want clean and positive energy, not a smoky room, so you can begin your Hoodoo workings.
- **Blessing the space.** Use infused liquids and dip a branch of your favorite tree to bless your space. Sprinkle the liquid from the branch and say a few words of blessing to strengthen the process.
- **Floor washes and sweeps.** Just like regular cleaning, this type of cleansing begins with the basics and cleans the surface of your space from negativity. Use a sweeping brush made from natural twigs to add intent to your process, and wash the floor with specially infused cleansers. Another way to freshen the area is to spread dried herbs around your floor – and then sweep them up. The energy they leave behind will stay with you until it's time to cleanse again.
- **Spritz the room.** Just like you used a spray to cleanse yourself, you can use a spray to concentrate your cleanse in certain parts of the space. Spritz your shrine or altar to give it a deep cleanse or spray around the doorway and windows to create strong barriers.
- **Diffusers.** Modern Hoodoo practitioners know that they can benefit from more modern methods of cleansing, and diffusers offer a balanced and safe method for getting the essence of their favorite herbs into the atmosphere. Essential oils are a fun and inexpensive way to bring the power of lemongrass, lavender, ylang-ylang, and all your favorite essences to your space.

- **Cleanse with light.** The sun's healing rays are a natural and effective way to clean your area. Don't sit in the dark; get those curtains open and let the power of solar energy flood your space. Open the windows and let all that stale and negative energy go. The sun will soon have those low-level entities heading for the hills.
- **Cleanse with sound.** Use bells and gongs to drive out negative energy. If you don't have any instruments, walk through your home from the front door to the back, clapping your hands, especially near the walls. Create a loop of energy in your home that you can fill with positivity by using sound and noise to create barriers.
- **Cleanse with salt.** Use Himalayan salt for a deep and pure cleanse. Sprinkle the salt at the doorway and on the sills of any windows. If you aren't a fan of the messy salt method, use a Himalayan salt lamp to bring the same energy.

As a routine, you should perform some form of self-cleanse at least once a week but especially after discord or arguments. If you feel a heavy atmosphere in your home, cleansing will help to lift spirits and create a calmer atmosphere.

How to Recognize If You Need a Cleanse

1. When you feel deep emotions without any explanation. Your mood swings from gleeful to deeply upset without any outside influences, and you feel affected by the smallest incidents.
2. Certain people make you feel drained or exhausted. You can't face them and actively avoid being in their company.
3. You need to shield yourself from the outside world. Feeling reluctant to leave the house and mix with other people is a clear sign that your energy levels are depleted. It isn't normal to isolate yourself and avoid company.
4. Your anxiety levels are on full alert. You constantly feel that you are in danger or that something is about to happen that won't be good for you.
5. You feel like somebody else's energy has invaded your mind or body. Do you feel haunted by someone else in your space or mind despite them not being there physically?

6. You are dogged by feelings of doom or negativity and see the worst in everything you see or feel. Evil seems like a part of your world, and you can't shake those feelings off.
7. Picking up other people's illnesses and health issues. If you begin to feel symptoms of illnesses you *don't have* but someone close to you *does have*, you are experiencing a transfer of energy from them, and you need a cleanse.
8. Other people's emotions and relationship issues infringe on your own emotions. If a friend of yours has a damaging breakup yet you feel the effects that aren't healthy and want to be of assistance to them, you need to cleanse your energy so you can be there for them.
9. Whenever you can't let go of arguments or conflicts, you are held back by your emotions and the energy they have created. Cleansing your energy will help you let go of past issues and resolve them by drawing a line in the sand.
10. When you feel something is off, but you don't know why.

Meditation Routines to Raise Your Vibrations

These simple meditation routines are designed to help with varying issues and target why you feel uncoordinated. Choose the one that speaks to you, and you will benefit from their tailored instructions.

Self-Forgiveness

For complete peace of mind, the first person you need to forgive is yourself. If you are holding on to negativity, you'll be unable to forgive others. Self-forgiveness is a precious gift you can give yourself. It brings peace to your spirit, transforms your life, and is helpful to those who come into your social circle.

For all your meditation, you need to find a space where you feel safe, calm, and able to express yourself without fear of being disturbed. Seat yourself on the floor and close your eyes before you focus on your intentions for five minutes. See your breath enter and leave your body and draw strength from it. Now picture yourself in your mind.

Think of what you have done to yourself to cause pain. Sometimes it can be helpful to imagine yourself in the third person and refer to yourself by your name. When you have a thought about the alternative, you and the harm they have caused throw the thought away as if it is a physical item.

What were the weaknesses that caused the alternative you to act like that? Was it a lack of self-awareness or emotional influences that made them act that way? Understand what fueled their behavior and why they did what they did. As your awareness grows, it will help you understand that, as humans, we are all flawed and that sometimes we expect too much. Tell yourself you forgive them and have let go of the pain they caused you. Tell them you forgive them, you understand why they acted as they did, and that you'll be more understanding and show more self-love in the future.

Relax for ten minutes and refocus on your breathing. Feel your emotions and spirit return to normal, and open your eyes. You should feel lighter and forgiven with a renewed understanding of your character and spirit.

The self-forgiveness meditation script can be adapted to work if you need to forgive others for the pain that they have caused you. Simply imagine their faces instead of your own and address the issues they have caused you. The process is cathartic, and you control the energy you bring to the experience. You can safely express your anger and frustration before letting it go forever.

A Healing Meditation Exercise

This exercise takes around seven minutes, including a minute at the end of the exercise, to relax and return to normal.

1. Sit or lie down in a comfortable place in a relaxing position.
2. Make your body completely still and relaxed.
3. Feel your muscles and limbs expand and grow longer as your body relaxes and softens.
4. Notice any additional sensations that are happening in your mind and body.
5. Ask yourself why you are feeling the things you are and how they make you react emotionally.
6. Listen to your body and the messages it is sending you.

7. Slow your breathing and let your focus rest on the air as it enters and leaves your lungs.
8. Close your mouth completely and breathe through your nose, taking notice of any changes to the messages this triggers.
9. Feel your abdomen rise and fall, and be aware of any sounds you make as you inhale and exhale.
10. Permit your body to declutter.
11. Name your breaths and breathe in love.
12. Breathe out tension.
13. Breathe in peace.
14. Breathe out anger.
15. Breathe in harmony.
16. Breathe out conflict.
17. Breathe in healing.
18. Breathe out illness.
19. Let your breath become deeper before you repeat the last exercise of inhaling and exhaling.
20. With the final breath, let out all self-judgment and criticism.
21. Breathe in love and joy.
22. Let your mind travel from the top of your head to the tips of your toes and heal your body.
23. Allow your body to share the energy equally and begin to heal.
24. Feel the here and now as you return to your conscious state.
25. Feel the silence for a minute before returning to your conscious life.

Inner Peace Meditation

Change your posture for this meditation to experience energy flow with your body shape. Sit in a comfortable place with your feet firmly on the floor approximately a foot in front of you. Let your knees relax and keep your ankles firm. Roll your shoulders to relax your posture, and then lower your chin to lengthen your neck.

Close your eyes and focus on your breaths. Take mindful breaths for a count of twenty and focus on the path the air takes. How are you feeling? What are your emotions and energy levels? Do you feel inner peace? Is there still turmoil? If you still feel unbalanced, repeat the breathing exercise. Is your body warm or cold? Relax and feel every sensation you can feel.

As you feel the peace descending, thank the spirits for their help and open your eyes slowly. Now begin to regain your normal senses and return to the waking world.

Harmony Meditation

Sit in a comfortable position where your back is supported, and you feel peaceful. Close your eyes and take a deep, meaningful breath.

Imagine a candle flickering brightly in your mind and allowing the flame's warmth to flow through your body, warming your aura. Let the warmth fill your soul and heart, and feel the glow reach your skin.

Keep your focus on the candle flame for as long as it feels comfortable, and bring your breath back to your focus. Remember to keep the glow of the candle in your heart as your eyes flicker open and you rejoin the world.

As you go about your daily routine, take the time to stop and reconnect with your inner candle to experience the harmony it holds for you.

When to Perform Cleansings

When should you cleanse your space? Every week, every month, or just when you feel the need? Here are some basic tips to help you craft your cleansing routine and make sure it works for you:

- **When there is a waning moon, cleanse your space.** When there is a new moon, cleanse your space. The natural energy will automatically cleanse your aura, but it needs to infiltrate your space, cleanse in the moonlight, and take advantage of the natural rays whenever you can.

- **Following illness, death, or serious misfortune in your home**. Has someone passed away or contracted a serious illness? Cleansing is essential to keep yourself immune, and you should cleanse both yourself and your space. If you perform rituals and spells to deal with the grief or to help the illness wane, you'll get better results with a positive space and attitude.

- **Always clear your space if you are collaborating with new spirits or deities.** You don't want residual energy sources to interfere with your connection, so cleanse yourself and your space, so you provide a blank canvas for their energy to impact upon.
- **After collaborating with new spirits and deities,** it's time for another cleanse. You don't want to bring any unfamiliar energies to your regular spirits, or they may rebel and start to pull away. The spirits need to know you respect them, and if you turn up with an aura or space soiled with unfamiliar energy, they may take offense.
- **Whenever visitors have left or if someone new moves into the home,** it will affect the spiritual balance of your space. Cleanse and restore the equilibrium before you start any rootwork or spells.

Chapter 5: Create a Hoodoo Shrine

What is a shrine? The definition says it is a place marked by its association with a sacred deity or relic and is a construction or building that people can visit to mark that respect. In Hoodoo, we recognize that deities and spirits are important, but worship can occur anywhere and at any time. It is an ongoing process, so your shrine has a different meaning in Hoodoo and can be whatever you like.

Your shrine could be constructed outdoors to improve your nature connection and show your respect for the powers of the natural world.
https://unsplash.com/photos/MnKWt1W1GDg

A shrine makes your work more resolute and focused; you can have as many as you like. Some practitioners have portable shrines they take with them when they travel, and others have dedicated shrines in their homes. A sacred space is a haven for you to return to where you know what is there and has a special place in your heart. Your shrine could be constructed outdoors to improve your nature connection and show your respect for the powers of the natural world. In this chapter, we will examine many forms of shrines, and you can then choose the one or more that suits your work.

A Portable Shrine

Keep it simple and choose a design that suits your style. You can be as decorative as you like and cover your shrine in stickers, symbols, and other decorative touches, or you can keep it neutral and inconspicuous to the outside world. If you are less keen to share your Hoodoo leanings with the world, the neutral option is best, but if you want to benefit from a dedicated shrine, the decorated item will suit you better.

Use the ideas below as a springboard for your own projects and a chance to get creative with your craft.

What You Need

- A box can be wooden, plastic, or any material you choose. An unfinished wooden box is more adaptable
- Sandpaper
- Cloths for cleaning
- Items relating to Hoodoo
- Small candles and holders
- Shells for offerings
- Small incense burner
- Craft items to decorate your box
- A protective spray to cover the finished product
- Paint or foil to cover your box
- Creative additions
- Woodburning tool for decoration

- Stickers and decals

Choose the symbols that relate to Hoodoo from the following

- **The triskelion**, or the triple whirl, is a symbol of magic and brings change to the interlocked energies in its form. It symbolizes spiritual, energetic, and material force and uses the power of the trio.
- **The pentagram** is the five-pointed star encased in a circle that represents the power of the four elements combined with the element of the spirit. The top point represents the strength of the deity and the divine, while the circle that surrounds the star is the ultimate barrier to unwanted energy and spirits. If you are creating the pentagram yourself, always draw it with a single stroke.
- **The spiral** is a universal symbol for all earthly needs. When it is drawn rotating to the right, it represents the power to summon material needs, while the spiraling left symbol deals with energies beyond the earthly planes and is also effective in dealing with illnesses and diseases.
- **The crossroads symbol** is representative of change and a need for new directions. It is used to help the user choose a path to walk and improve their life.
- **The Star of David** is a hexagram with the compound of two equilateral triangles and was used as the seal of Solomon in the Bible. In Hoodoo workings, it is a powerful protection symbol that can be used to keep out negative energies and spirits.

Hoodoo Items for Your Portable Shrine

- Curios like a coin, lodestones, or animal bones
- Incense for luck or love
- Powders you may use
- Lucky oil
- A rabbit's foot for luck
- John the Conqueror root

Decorate Your Box

Paint or varnish your box ready for your decoration and then use your imagination to make the box a part of your personality and something you'll enjoy for years. Make sure you create a solid seal or locking device, as your loose items will be stored inside. Use ribbons or stoppers to ensure your box's lid forms an L-shaped surface for your work when you are away from home.

Think about where and when you will use your shine and how to utilize your limited space. Your portable shrine should be available to go at a second's notice, so make sure it is easy to stash away in your home and can be reached easily when you need to go.

Ancestors Shrine

Our ancestors hold a sacred place in Hoodoo beliefs, and a shrine dedicated to them makes your work more intense and fueled by their influence. A shrine to your ancestors can be constructed anywhere in the home where visitors can admire and respect it. Asian and Eastern cultures believe that shrines to the dead should be part of the entrance space in their homes, so they are one of the first things visitors see.

Use pictures of your relatives and items they once owned to decorate a small table covered with a rich gold cloth. Place candles and incense sticks at the side of their portrait pictures and light them whenever you send a request to the spirits. Add an offering bowl so you can gift them with tokens of your respect and love. Clear a space for your additional offerings, like a glass of wine or a piece of homemade bread. A bowl of their favorite sweets or a piece of cake is symbolic of your love and will feed their energies and yours. Place a bowl on your shrine that represents their lineage and the connection that they have to you. Add a small amount of cool water, a drop of your favorite scent, some of your bodily fluid - a tear or a small drop of sweat. Now dedicate the shrine to the spirits by saying a small prayer and sprinkling the liquid across the shrine.

Whenever you replace the water or other elements of the shrine, remember to name any ancestors that you are aware of and acknowledge the ones you cannot name due to a lack of knowledge. Offer your gifts to your ancestors and the spirits that reside with them so they will band together and become part of your spiritual team.

A Living Shrine Dedicated to Nature

Suppose you have a spacious garden or a space. In that case, you can construct a living shrine to nature and benefit from the energies created by performing your rituals and spells outside. Use natural materials to create a sacred place to perform your spells; stone and wood are readily available and extremely durable. Use plants to decorate your shrine and create a tranquil place – yet one filled with living energy.

If possible, incorporate a water feature in your shrine so you'll benefit from the natural force of running water. Represent the four elements on your shrine in the most natural forms you can find. A wind chime represents air, water features for water, plants represent the earth and candles for the element fire. Remember that your shrine will change as the seasons progress, and you can replace items that appear as the year progresses.

A More Traditional Shrine for Your Home

Concentrating on a space in your home where you can practice and perform your spells is an intensely personal experience and depend on several factors. The size of your home, the area you have to work with, and how secret you want your shrine to be are just a few.

The most important part of your decision is how permanent your shrine will be. If you must move it every time you finish your work, this will affect how elaborate your shrine can be. A better alternative for you could be a series of portable shrines that you can use whenever you like. The instructions below are more dedicated to those of you that have the space for a permanent shrine and how to use the space to create a sacred place for your Hoodoo work.

Choose Your Space

Ideally, the surface of your shrine should be level with your waist or higher. You don't want prying hands and eyes to have access to your sacred space, and you want to avoid family pets disturbing your items. Try a regular table in your chosen space to see if it works for you before you start constructing your ornate shrine.

Create the Shrine

You should build your shrine from scratch if you are good with your hands. Create a solid and decorative structure that has multiple levels to place your special items and dedicated offerings to the spirits and nature.

If you want a simpler multi-level shrine, a coffee table or TV stand works well and sits well in most spaces. Another alternative shrine space is a cupboard mounted on the wall. The shelves work well for multi-functional offerings, and the doors mean you can shut the shrine away until you are ready to use it once more. The key thing to consider is that whatever your chosen shrine was in a former life, it has now become redundant. You can't use a coffee table as a shrine one day and as a table the next. Your shrine should be sacred and not multi-functional. Once you have blessed it and dedicated it to your Hoodoo work, it should stay in shrine mode from that moment.

Decorate Your Shrine

Choose a cloth to cover the surface and place a representative object of each of the four elements in the corners. A feather from a bird represents air, a stone represents the earth, a seashell represents water, and a candle represents fire.

Add bowls for your offerings. Ideally, they should be made from natural substances and differ in size to hold varying offerings you may place there. Add a cup and glass for liquid offerings and a coaster or plate for holding heated elements.

Add symbolic shapes to your shrine and pictures of the deities you follow. A cross or a star of Bethlehem represents Christ, and you can include religious icons if your faith is strong. Your shrine is a celebratory way to connect to the spirits, and how you decorate it is a strong statement to the spirit world that you believe in. What you believe is the power that makes you a magical being and gives you the strength to operate as such.

Add Light to Your Shrine

It should be a wondrous place filled with positivity and hope. Lights bring that energy. Use candles, lamps, and reflective surfaces to light the darkness and illuminate your soul. Some candles have special wicks that crackle as they burn to add the element of sound to your work. Use additional light sources around the rest of the room to make the shrine bathed in light whenever you use it.

Engage the Senses

Your shrine should be interactive. Including all your senses will make your work more comprehensive and powerful. Bells are a perfect way to bring sound to your work, and you should find decorative bells with differing tones to bring music to your shrine. You could have a CD player or another form of music source so you can record pertinent music for your work or record your mantras to play as you work.

Incense and perfumes will enhance your shrine and bring your sense of smell to life. Incense brings energy and intention, and it smells great so use it whenever you can.

You can represent the sense of touch with tactile objects for your shrine, like prayer beads and other pleasantly shaped objects. Include a decorative cushion for seated activities or a soft and welcoming wrap to wear around your shoulders. A rug to stand on will help you become grounded and leave your excess energies behind when you finish your work.

Key Things to Consider about Your Shrine

- Your home shrine is a sacred space and should be treated as such. Tell your family and friends that it is your space, and they shouldn't invade it. Don't use the space for functional uses. You will only diminish the space and make it less sacred. The objects on your shrine are blessed, and moving them will only make them mundane and lose their power.

- Replace fresh items regularly. If you have a bowl of water or fresh flowers on your shrine, you should never let them decay and rot. Fresh energy comes from living sources, while any sign of neglect will affect your work and bring negativity.

- Make sure your shrine is in a safe space away from drafts and chilly air. You should treat the shrine as a living object of your faith and ensure it is comfortable and able to breathe.

- Cleanse the area regularly with normal cleaning routines as well as spiritual ones. Smudge the area with sage and use blessed water to sprinkle on it. Dust and dirt will only bring negativity to your space, so clean it thoroughly and with care as if it was a temple.

Your shrine is your sacred space and should be the crucial point of your magical life. Use the space to create magic but also to regenerate your energies. Visit it whenever you need to be reminded of your connection to the spirits and the joy and love they bring to your life.

You can have multiple shrines in your life to represent varying events. You could have a small shrine to mark the passing of your favorite pet that marks where they are buried. Shrines will often be built for the ashes of a loved one to rest upon and for the people who miss them to connect to their spirits. You may prefer a mental shrine to your Hoodoo beliefs, a mind palace filled with your wildest dreams and expectations. A mind palace doesn't cost a penny and can be taken with you wherever you go. You can store information, images, and other relevant information to make you a better magician and conjuror. Fill your mind place with the knowledge of your ancestors and add to their wisdom with quotes and inspiration from more traditional sources from the origins of Hoodoo.

Create a Mind Palace as a Shrine

1. Choose a place to feature in your mind palace. This can be a place already known to you or a completely unique environment. It could be your home or a place you felt safe as a child.
2. Note the distinctive features. What do you see that makes you comfortable and instinctively marks the place where you are? It can be furniture or scenery. It could be a smell or familiar scent that identifies the spot you are in. Every piece of your mind palace will contain relevance so make sure you take the time to note them all and the significance they hold.
3. Remember the details by writing them down and committing them to memory.
4. When you revisit your mind palace, always enter the environment from the same direction, so the place looks the same.
5. Fill your mind palace with the tools of your craft, and remember that the magic you create will be just as relevant as

your physical work. You have a place you can experiment with your Hoodoo, and no one will disturb you.

A mind palace is normally a place you can go to improve your memory, but if you don't have the luxury of building a regular shrine to your beliefs, it provides you with a sacred space you can escape to. Hoodoo and magic are all about embracing ideas and building on them. This psychological exercise could become the most important part of your landscape and give you a chance to grow and expand your spiritual being.

Another way to create a shrine without physical space is to use online resources to create your place of peace. An online shrine can be another extension of your imagination with boundless access to amazing resources. You can create a place of wonder with just a couple of clicks of your mouse. Online shrines travel with you and are just a tap of a button away. You can create online icons and elaborately write your petitions to make your shrine a tribute to your imagination and skills. You don't have to be a tech wizard to create online magic. You just need access to a PC or a similar smart device and the Internet.

FAQS about Shrines

Can I have more than one shrine?

Of course, you can. The limit on how many you have is for you to decide. If you travel down the mind palace shrine option, you can create as many as you like, as the possibilities are endless. You can create a shrine to the African people who lived and breathed Hoodoo or a shrine to the people who join you on your quest in the modern world. Your shrines can be physical, mental, and even online.

Can a shrine be dedicated to both spirits and ancestors?

Yes. You have a spiritual team dedicated to you and who work together to bring magic and love to your life. Your ancestors are just a part of that team and if you want to include them and the spirits within your shrine, just do it. Remember to name them when you give thanks, and they will be satisfied with your efforts.

Can a shrine be dedicated to more than one ancestor?

Again yes, if you had a shrine for every ancestor, your home would be filled with them. Your ancestors are your life's blood, and they understand that they have all contributed to your life.

Should I include relatives in my shrine?

As nouns, the difference between ancestors and relatives is that ancestors are from your direct bloodline, while relatives are someone connected by marriage or blood ties. Does this make them less significant? Surely the person your grandfather married had an equal part to play in creating the person you call your father. It's your call. Ancestors, forefathers, and progenitors are all significant, but all relatives have played a part in the amazing person you are today.

Chapter 6: Hoodoo Candles and Bottles

Candles and bottles are an intrinsic part of Hoodoo magic. They were always readily available in slave households, so using them in their spells and rituals made sense. Candles didn't just bring light and warmth to the home. They provided an inexpensive magical tool for use by all ages. Today we can all use candles to create magic and learn the correct way to use these simple items to create impressive results.

Candles and bottles are an intrinsic part of Hoodoo magic.
https://www.pexels.com/photo/red-pillar-candle-with-black-background-6129843/

Candle Colors

Just like choosing the color of your mojo bags, the color of the candles you use influences your work from the very start. They set your intention and work with the other elements you choose to create a strong bond with the spirits and ensure success. The meaning of the colors in candle magic is slightly different from the mojo bags, so it is worth reexamining them and what they signify.

- **Black**: The occult and dark magic, removal of negativity and binding with the night. The womb and feminine power, especially in relationships.
- **White**: Angelic connections, purity, freedom of spirit, transformation, and rebirth.
- **Red**: Courage and strength in combat, anger, fire, lust, and sex. Red also represents the passion for relationships and your career.
- **Orange**: Control in legal matters, opportunities, harvesting, and also power over your enemies.
- **Blue**: Communication and mental clarity. The healing power of water and dreams.
- **Purple**: Spiritual awakening, magic, intuitive powers, wisdom, and knowledge.
- **Yellow**: The color of the sun, joy, love, and peace. Creativity and inspiration it is the color of success.
- **Green**: Abundance and wealth. Green is the color of the earth and fertility and represents money and love.
- **Pink**: Self-confidence and love, friendships and relationships, emotional healing, and harmony.
- **Brown**: Animal connections, grounding, and focusing on your emotions. Recovering lost items and security.

Types of Candles and What They Represent

- **Tealights** are small colorful candles that are sometimes scented and often come in packs with multiple color options. They don't burn for long and are found in most dollar stores and discount outlets. Use these for your first few spells to ensure that candle magic is right for you before investing in more elaborate options.

- **Birthday candles** are another cheap and cheerful option; these are taller than tea lights and can be used as a quick-burning substitute for regular candles.
- **Tapers** are long thin candles you probably saw in your grandmother's home; their shape makes them perfect for altar work and for sealing your bottles with wax.
- **Novenas** are for working with selected religious figures. They are decorated with pictures of saints or other leading religious figures. Specialist stores have extended novenas to include more varied deities and spirits, and if you want to work with specific deities, they can commission candles just for you.
- **The 7-knob candle** is part of African American folklore and is designed for extended spells that take place over the seven days of the week. Light each knob daily and let them burn until the week has ended and the spell is complete.
- **Pillar candles** come in a range of sizes and burn for hours. They are perfect for lighting your shrine and honoring your ancestors.
- **Figure candles** are more specialized and represent whatever they are modeled on. There are figure candles featuring male and female forms and a couple's candle for spells regarding relationships. Animal candles help you connect with animal spirit guides and familiars.
- **Floating candles** are especially effective when used in conjunction with other water elements. They also work well when working with fire elements as they create spiritual polarity.

Candles need to be charged to work in spells and rituals, which involves dressing the candle and then charging it with your energy. Dressing a candle is a skill you'll learn as your experience grows, but here are a few simple tips to start with:

1. Use a knife or a pin to carve your intentions into the candle. Use short, powerful words to indicate what you want from the magic, and your requests will be heard more clearly.
2. Anoint the candle in oil, choose an oil representing your intentions and coat the candle in your chosen oil.
3. Coat the candle with herbs and powders to make it more effective. Lay the herbs and powders on a wooden board and gently roll the anointed candle until it is covered.
4. Load your candle by carving a small portion out of the top of the candle and loading oil or herbs to create a concentrated section.
5. Scatter herbs, oil, crystal, and talismans around the base of the candle to intensify your intentions.

Safety Tips for Candle Work

- Never leave the candle unattended
- Don't overload your candles. Just a pinch of herbs and plant matter will make sure you don't pose a fire risk.

Charging Your Candle

When you are beginning to understand Hoodoo, you'll encounter the term "charging" a lot. What does it mean? Simply put, you transmit your energy into the tools and items you work with. The charge comes from the electricity supply when you charge your electrical devices. In Hoodoo, *you are the power source.* Your visualization powers, and your sheer will, coupled with desire, will charge your items with a power that makes electricity seem lame.

Cast a Basic Candle Spell

So now that you have the basics, it's up to you to create a signature style that works for you. Most rituals and spells follow the pattern listed below:

1. Choose the type and color of your candle.
2. Add the oils and herbs to the board, ready for charging.
3. Use a sharp tool to carve your intentions and sigils into the candle.

4. Start to visualize your intentions and how they will manifest.
5. Anoint the candle.
6. Dress the candle.
7. Light it and let the candle burn down naturally. This is recommended for beginners, so they don't snuff out the candle prematurely and halt the spell.
8. Dispose of the remnants.

How to Dispose of Candle Remnants

This all depends on your intentions. If you cast a spell to draw something to you, then bag the remnants and keep them close, in your wardrobe or under your bed. If the spell was a banishing spell, then dispose of the elements in a natural source like running water or fire. If you can't do that, then throw them in the trash on the other side of town. The further away, the better.

Ceromancy

The fine art of candle reading is one of the world's oldest forms of divination, and learning to read what the candles are telling you will add to your psychic skills and improve your understanding of the spiritual world.

Reading the flame is the natural way to practice ceromancy and is a simple way to begin using this particular art. When you light the candle, the initial smoke that is created is the first sign of ceromancy. If the smoke is white, it means your answers will come immediately, and black smoke means they will come, but there will be obstacles. If the flame doesn't smoke, it can mean the matter is now irrelevant and has been dealt with. The strength of your flame also indicates the strength of your success. A robust bright flame bodes well, while a weak and low flame shows opposition to your petition.

Stare at the flame for a more in-depth reading from your candle. If the center of the flame is a blazing red color, it means you'll get a resolution for your needs, while a dimmer light indicates you must work for your results. Suppose the candle's wick is forming a bulb shape. In that case, it indicates that a third party is working against you, and you need to remove their negative energy.

If your candle's flame is spitting, popping, and behaving erratically, it strongly signifies that you have forces working against you. Listen to your instincts and if you feel the flame is growing uncomfortably, then extinguish the flame; if you gain a feeling of security from the conflict, sit back and enjoy the light show.

Burning candles for love follows a different set of rules. If you burn a single candle and a secondary flame rises from the ashes or the wax remnants, it means you have a rival. If you want to discover your relationship status with ceromancy, then burn two candles side by side; one represents you and the other your partner. Suppose one candle burns away significantly quicker than the other. In that case, it signifies an imbalance in the relationship and suggests that it won't last or needs serious attention.

Wax Readings and What They Mean

Reading the wax left by a burning candle is an art similar to reading tea leaves. The shapes and images created by the wax indicate what the candle is trying to tell you. However, how the candle burns is also a significant way to obtain information. If the candle burns down on one significant side, your issues haven't been resolved. Try the process again with a different candle if you get the same result something or someone is standing in your way.

As the candle burns, you will notice tears forming in the wax. If they melt away naturally, the omens are good for your spell, but if they harden on the side of the candle, you are experiencing bad luck, and your spell will be ineffective. The sides of the candle represent different areas of your life; the front is the material world and represents your health, prosperity, and your home. The back of the candle represents the spiritual and emotional world and will indicate how your energies are in this realm. The right side is the future, and the left side is the past.

The shapes formed by the wax as it solidifies are called "persistent" images, which indicate how the spell has worked. If spells for love are cast, and the persistent image resembles a heart, this is a good sign. If you are burning a money spell and the image resembles a coin or a bill, it looks good for your spell.

Enclosed candles are a powerful part of Hoodoo rituals when a candle is placed in a bell jar and left to burn. The residue left on the glass provides further clues, and the color of the soot created by the candle is also significant. If soot appears at the top half of your candle, you have successfully resolved any obstacles. If the soot is at the bottom of the candle, you still have unfinished business. White soot anywhere in the jar is a positive sign from the spirits that all is well.

Wax on Water Divination

To answer your questions clearly, you should use candles to get clear indications from the spirit.

What you need

- Scrying bowl: This is a bowl to store your water and use it to cast your wax. Natural materials are best, like glass, ceramic, or wood but avoid using plastic or metal containers.
- Fresh water.
- Candle/s and lighter, white candles work, but colored candles cast more focused intentions.
- Pencil and paper to write the answers down.
- Oil.

Choose a calm space to place your bowl and sit next to it. Fill the bowl with water and take a few minutes to compose your mind. If you use oil to anoint the candle, take three drops of the same oil and put it in the water. This will charge your water and make your intentions stronger. Write your question or your petition on the paper and set it to one side. Take time to reiterate your question in your mind before you start the ritual.

Light the candle and hold it vertically over the water until a good amount of wax has formed. Now tilt the candle and set the tip an inch above the water. Let the molten wax flow into the water, and continue to ask your question. Be patient and let the wax form a nice pool rather than random drips. Don't interfere or move the bowl or the candle but let the wax and water blend naturally.

The wax will naturally move and form shapes, and you can observe the interactions between the two elements. Once you feel the process has reached a natural end, snuff out the candle and observe what the wax tells you. At this point, it is important to understand that there are no right and wrong ways to interpret wax readings. They will speak to you and form images to answer your questions because they are controlled by natural forces working with you.

Have fun with your readings; remember, the wax is there for you, and you'll see what you need to see.

Bottle Magic

Perhaps the most popular form of Hoodoo bottle magic is the bottle tree. Bottle trees originated back in West Africa in the 9th century and traveled to the US with the communities of people brought to these shores from West Africa during the slavery era. The Hoodoo belief uses bottle trees to keep marauding spirits and nocturnal entities from entering the home and creating havoc. The idea is that the bottles will be too interesting and shiny for the spirits to ignore, and they will be tricked into entering the bottle to check it out. They then become trapped in the bottle so the householder can cork the bottle and get rid of them. The sunlight will destroy nocturnal spirits but if you aren't sure, cast the bottle into the water to ensure they are destroyed completely. As all Hoodoo practitioners know, evil spirits hate sunlight and water.

Bottle trees are also used to commemorate the dead and honor the ancestors. The traditional blue bottles represent the color of heaven, where the ancestors reside. Use a basic bottle tree and adorn it with shiny, eye-catching vessels and household items. Add cups, bowls, knives, forks, and different colored bottles to make your tree beautiful and impressive.

Bottle Spells

You can use many different bottle spells, but here are a few that are more specific and will give you an idea of how to use bottle magic in your Hoodoo work.

The Boss Fix Bottle Spell
What You Need

- One white candle approx. 4" long
- Candle holder in the shape of a star
- Blessed High John oil
- Herb mix including sage, parsley, garlic, and anise
- A sheet of paper and a pen
- A small jar of honey

- An empty bottle

Take the parchment paper and list everything you dislike about your boss and co-workers. Place it in the bottle. Add the honey, oil, and herb to the candle by dressing it. Burn the candle down as you ask the spirits for their help to make things better at work. Add the honey to the bottle, and when the candle has burned down, add the wax and ashes to the honey. Seal the bottle and place it in a dark space. The requests you have made will soon be met.

A Business Spell Bottle or Jar
What You Need

- White sand
- Mint leaves
- Rose petals
- Cardamom pods
- Crystalized ginger
- Paper and pen

Write your intentions on the paper. "I ask the spirits for their assistance in making my business thrive. I will work hard and bring my positivity, and I ask that they do the same. Thank you."

Add the paper and the other items except for the sand to the bottle and then fill it with the sand. Bless the bottle with your intentions and place it on your shrine.

Spell Jars

Spell jars are another way to cast your intentions and create protective and powerful spells that last. When you use jars, they give you a choice of size, meaning they can come with you when you travel or remain in the home to bring their magic.

Jar spells are generally based on strong intentions and corresponding ingredients. These include the following

- Personal items like fingernails, photos, hair, or a piece of paper with their name on it.
- Written intentions on a piece of paper asking for the spirits to come to your assistance and what you require from the

magic.
- Liquids to fill the jar, including vinegar for banishing, urine for breaking a curse, honey and nectar for compulsion, and tinctures that contain your intentions.
- Solids like rusty nails or broken glass to break a curse. Cat hair and dog hair break a couple up, so they fight like "cats and dogs," but beware, the spell can backfire. Money-related spells should involve coins or banknotes, while love spells use ribbons or glitter to represent the joy of love.

Crystals and Herbs for Specific Intentions

Feel free to add this list to your ingredient section to intensify your knowledge and source of reference:

- **Intent banishing** uses obsidian, black tourmaline, quartz, and jet as crystals and clove dragons' blood and garlic as herbs.
- **For binding spells,** combine jet with knotweed and hazel or spiderwort when available.
- **For improved communication,** use turquoise and tiger eye crystals with mint or orris root.
- **Curse breaking** uses onyx, selenite, and clear quartz with salt, sage, and rue.
- **Fertility** spells use agate, emeralds, peridot, and ivy.
- **Health** spells use agate, jade, and sunstone with galangal root, rosemary, sage, and thyme.
- **Knowledge** spells involve fluorite and nutmeg, and rosemary.
- **Love** spells require amber, rose quartz, and emerald combined with Adam and Eve root, rose, laurel clove, and lavender.
- **Money** spells use gold, malachite, and moss with ginger, citrus vervain, and patchouli.
- **Peace** spells use blue agate, silver, and amazonite with lavender, violet, and sage.
- **Productivity** spells are fueled by gold, ruby, and hematite with allspice and vanilla.

- **Protection** spells use amber, sandalwood, malachite, and citrine combined with salt, angelica, and mugwort.
- **Psychic connections** use jet, malachite, silver, and turquoise with yarrow as acacia.
- **Relationships** involve pearl and agate with sapphire and turquoise and agate with pansy and rose.

Sealing Your Jar

Once you have chosen your ingredients, add them to your jar and cast a mantra to seal your intentions. It doesn't have to be fancy. Your words are the power behind the spell. Try something like this "I call on the power of the elements to help me find love. I ask for the magic energy of the rose and the goddesses to bring me true passion and help me find my soulmate. Thank you for your consideration and energy."

Now use a candle to seal your jar. You can use ribbons and other methods, but candles are spectacular and add intent to your jar. Place a correctly colored candle on the lid of your jar and let it burn down completely so the wax covers the lid and effectively seals it. You can burn additional candles to recharge your jar spell later or multiple candles in the first instance.

Chapter 7: How to Make Mojo Bags

A mojo bag is a must-have accessory in Hoodoo circles. They are colorful small bags filled with things that keep you safe, keep you connected to your roots, and give you a sense of connection to the spiritual world. Your mojo bag is a personal piece of kit and should never be handled by anybody else just in case their energy interferes with the intention you invest in your bag.

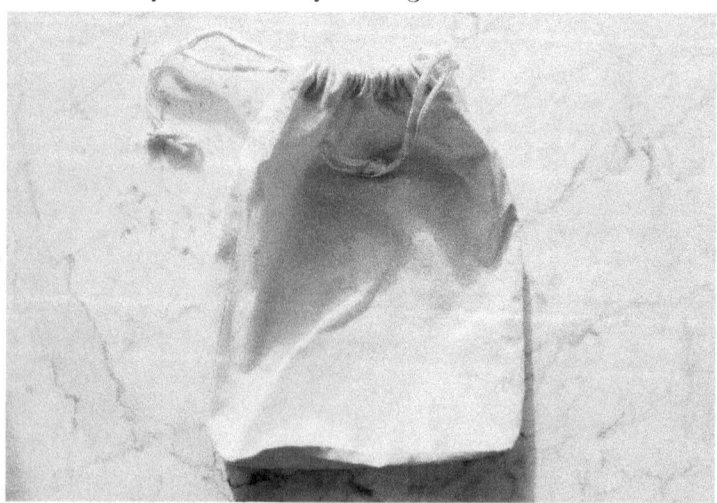

A mojo bag is a must-have accessory in Hoodoo circles.
https://www.pexels.com/photo/white-textile-bag-with-drawstrings-placed-on-marble-table-3850465/

You can create mojo bags for all your needs by customizing the ingredients and the colors you use. A bag for love will help you set your intention to find a new partner, while a money-based mojo bag will attract wealth and prosperity. Choose each element of your bag to make them into powerful, easy-to-make bags of magic that can be carried on your person or left on your shrine to recharge when they aren't needed.

Choose the Color of Your Bags

Why is color so important? We know that vibrations fuel the universe and life, and colors are an elevated expression of these vibrations. Hoodoo uses the power of colors in candle work, potions, spells, and all forms of magic, so mojo bags are directly affected by the color of the cloth chosen.

White

A white mojo bag is the ultimate part of your magic tools and ingredients, as it can be used when other colors aren't available. It is the color of purity and protection and has associations with the Moon and the zodiac sign Cancer. It brings light to dark spaces and imbues the holder with spirituality, peace of mind, and soul. White is especially protective of the young and represents their elemental purity and innocence. It neutralizes negativity, ill feelings, brings healing energies to your magic, and repairs both physical and psychic wounds.

Yellow

The color of the sun, the bringer of life, and the warmth of the universe. It is a happy color that represents the color of wheat and its importance in our daily life. Its golden hue also brings energy and love to you, and it improves vigor and energy for those who are depleted and run down. Yellow bags help creative people find inspiration and flourish in their fields. It symbolizes knowledge and happiness.

Orange

The color of Buddhism, orange, symbolizes health and helps the holder fight depression and sadness. It is a gentler form of energy than red, but it stimulates you without the violent energy that forms the color of fire. Orange is soothing yet invigorating and is the balancing point between the blood life of red and the mind intellect of yellow.

Use an orange cloth to promote success and power alongside friendship and positive events in your life. It brings success without any casualties and helps you overcome your inhibitions and social conditioning. It is the color of the setting sun and reminds us to connect to nature and reap the rewards.

Red

The color of love, red, is also the most powerful color for a mojo bag. The ingredients you add will set the intentions so that the outer bag could hold some explosive surprises. You need to be careful when using red bags, they can burn anyone who isn't prepared for their energy, and they can become destructive in the wrong hands. Use red to attract sexual energy and passion and to express your self-belief to the spiritual world. It can be therapeutic for people who have lost their inner strength, but if they are anxious or nervous, it can be too much for them to handle, and they should choose yellow or orange instead.

Pink

Often referred to as a female color, pink is actually quite powerful for both sexes. It is a calming color that attracts friendship and genuine affection. It can solve disputes and strengthen relationships, especially for shy people who are less likely to form relationships naturally. A pink mojo bag will give you the confidence to express yourself without worrying about what other people think.

Purple

The color of regality, this deep shade is associated with the Moon and is a symbol of spirituality and morals. It attracts spirit guides, helps you connect to your enigmatic side, and intensifies your psychic powers. Use a purple bag to protect yourself from psychic attacks and negative energy. As the true color of energy, it will help you find peace and increase your powers of devotion. Keep items you use in rituals in purple bags to keep them strong and intensified with positivity.

Green

The color of the planet Venus, this verdant shade is associated with Mother Earth and nature and gives you the strength of rebirth and creation. It is especially effective for money-based bags and brings prosperity and growth to the objects inside and the wearer. Green inspires creativity and growth and protects the holder from envy and jealousy. Green mojo bags are linked to the earth, the natural cycle of seasons, and the power of the harvest. It is a strong standalone color of a mojo bag and should never be mixed with a red bag; the balance of both colors would be disrupted and lead to miscommunication and possibly misplaced and dangerous magic effects.

Black

The color of funerals and death, black, is probably the most misunderstood color of the spectrum. It is associated with Saturn and brings protective energy that is both powerful and nourishing. It provides a shield from evil and a primordial unity that gives the holder strength to join the universe and benefit from its energy.

Blue

The color of Jupiter, blue, is the symbol of inner peace and meditative energy. It brings calm, healing energy to you and helps when you need to quit your domestic situation and stop the noise. Use it to create reconciliations and restore love and harmony to your life. Blue works well with other colors and can be used as a catalyst for other energetic forces.

Brown

The color of the earth – don't be fooled into thinking this drab hue is lacking in power when used for mojo bags. It is a staple color of nature and provides security and tenacity, which is just as magnificent as the trunk of a mighty oak tree. Brown is safe and will keep you protected from legal matters and injustices while solving your material issues.

What Materials Should You Use for Your Bags?

The choice is yours. The most practical bags are cotton or a polyester mix to provide a cheap yet durable source of the material. You can use recycled cloth to make your bags. In this way, you are connecting to your past and telling nature you recognize the power of recycling. Some bags will be especially dear to your heart, and you can mark that fact by using rich and expensive materials like velvet and silk. You must treasure these materials and only use them for your highly prized mojo bags.

The instructions below show you how to make a simple mojo bag that you can fill with your magic items to give them the power to work. Use this template for your bags to ensure they are durable and will withstand the refueling that is a natural process of owning a mojo bag.

How to Make a Basic Bag

1. Cut a square of your chosen material.
2. Form a pouch that is big enough to hold your chosen items.
3. Stitch the sides with strong yarn.
4. Fold over the edges to form a place to thread a drawstring.
5. Add the string to close the bag once you have your items inside.

You can also take a rectangular piece of material and simply draw the edges together while your items are already in the center. Take a piece of string and secure the edges of the bag with it. These bags are less fiddly to make and aren't meant to be opened at any time. The items in them should be chosen to stay there for a long time and shouldn't be fresh or prone to degrading.

Items You Can Include in Your Bags

Most basic bags have at least three items and never more than thirteen. The number of items you include should always be odd, and an even number will bring you bad luck or render the bag ineffective. The items you include can be as simple as the following:

- A personal item or a representation of yourself like a fingernail, a lock of your hair, or blood.
- A petition to the spirits that states what you require if you want a specific outcome.
- Herbs or minerals that show your intention.
- A talisman or coin.
- Trinkets from nature, like a seashell or twig from a tree.
- Jewelry.
- Keys.
- Dirt or soil from your favorite place.

Every item you place in your bag should be chosen carefully and have a specific purpose. Don't mix your intentions; focus on what you want to achieve with each mojo bag, and avoid muddying your spiritual intentions.

Here are some common items you can choose and what they represent:

- The Ace of Spades playing card - for good luck in gambling matters.
- An arrowhead for love and security.
- Black hair from a cat to break up relationships and bring prosperity from gambling.
- Black hair from a dog to create trouble for your enemies and break up their relationships.
- Black salt for protection and cleansing.
- Brick dust for good luck in business and financial matters.
- Copper coins for luck and prosperity.
- Lucky charms like a horseshoe.
- Business card for improved business luck or better communication
- A picture of your intended mate to ensure love is part of your relationship.
- Seashells represent your connection to nature.
- Lodestones for love.
- Crystals for fixed intentions.
- Earth from your garden for healing.
- Herbs and roots.

Of course, the list is endless. Providing you feel a connection to an item, it can be added to your mojo bag. Now that you have the contents of your bag, it's time to bless them before you seal the bag for good.

Light a candle in a color that represents your intent. For example, a mojo bag for luck would be blessed with a green candle. Now give your bag a name that represents its intent. For luck, you may call it Chance or Shiva, which represents the power of luck.

Now add your items while reciting the following,

"May you bring me a light in the dark,

May you give me the luck and fulfillment my life desires,

Stay by my side (add name) and be my sweet companion,

I feel safe in your company, and I trust my vision will be enhanced,

Luck be with me, and luck is my fate. "

Now Feed Your Bag

Just like a living object, the bag needs to be nurtured. The most common options are oils that have been blessed or water that has been charged by the moon or sun. Some Hoodoo workers use whisky, while others use Florida water. Once again, the choice is yours. Using bodily fluids is an option but be careful who you share your choices with.

Breathe Life into Your Bag

Hold the bag in the palm of your hand and give out three short breaths to give it life and connect it to your inner psyche.

Charge Your Bag

Keep the bag next to your skin for seven whole days to charge it with your intentions. Keep it in your underwear or a pocket beneath your clothes. When you sleep, keep it in your nightwear or in the pillowcase you sleep on. The only time it isn't with you should be when you are showering or in the bath. Your bag should be with you whenever you leave the house.

Charging your bag is an ongoing process; you should feed it monthly and charge it whenever possible. It should be as normal as picking up your house keys whenever you leave your home, and if you leave your bag behind, you should feel naked and like something is missing.

Your mojo bag is a living, breathing extension of your spirit and needs to be kept healthy. Some people believe they should always be accessible, while others think they should be sealed forever. Again, the choice is yours.

Ideas for Your Initial Mojo Bags

As beginners, it can be intimidating to make your first mojo bag. Will I get it right, and will it be effective for me? These are questions that most inexperienced Hoodoo workers will ask. The first thing to realize is that you can't cause any harm with your bags; the worst thing that can happen is that they don't work because they have mixed energies and send out the wrong message to the spirits. You should see results almost immediately by keeping it simple with your first bags.

These examples will give you an idea of how to use simple ingredients to create a powerful mojo bag:

Financial Mojo Bag: Used to attract wealth, prosperity, and money to your life

Choose a green cloth to fashion your bag and gold or black string to fasten it. Select some herbs to add to your bag; bay leaves, thyme, and laurel all work well. Add something that represents your intentions. If you want fast cash, then show your hand by adding a banknote or a coin to your ingredients. Now write your intention on a piece of paper, an amount you need, or a specific way you want your wealth to improve and add that to the pile.

These three items are a perfect way to power a money bag, but you can add your own representations depending on your feel for the bag. Once you have sealed the bag, feed it with smoke from incense or essential oil to activate your bag before you say a prayer or a mantra to bless it. Name your bag with a suitable word. Rich works if you want a powerful name or something more subtle like Penny or Will.

Keep the bag with you for at least seven days, and then use it whenever needed to improve your financial status. Imagine money flowing toward you whenever you feel the need, and your wishes will come true very soon.

Love Mojo Bag

Are you looking for new love, or do you want to get your ex back? Are you ready for love to be part of your life and want to give yourself more chances with a powerful mojo bag to hurry along the process?

Choose a red or pink cloth depending on the strength of the passion you want to attract. If you want to meet someone and gradually fall in love, then pink will work for you, but if you want a grand passion that lights up your life and makes your toes curl, then red is the cloth for you.

Add herbs that symbolize your desires. Cardamom seeds or rose petals will bring love, while lovage roots and myrtle are a powerful attraction for passion. Add a love token like a carved heart or a picture of the object of your desire. If you don't have specific intentions, then write a petition for love on a piece of red paper instead. Crystals that are red or pink are another strong ingredient and can be added but don't forget to keep the number of your items to odd numbers.

Charge the bag with rose essential oil or smudge it with incense before you say a short prayer or mantra over your bag. Carry it with you to charge it, and then keep it close whenever you are looking for love.

Mojo bags are for every part of your life, and you can never have too many. Keep them close to you whenever you need them by wearing them against your skin. If you find your bag isn't working as well as it used to, then dispose of it and replace it with a new one. Be respectful when you dispose of your bag, and make sure the old ingredients are thanked for their use and then buried or burned ceremoniously. All your magical ingredients should be respected and honored even when they have lost their power; they have served you well and deserve recognition.

Chapter 8: The Magic Practices of Rootwork

Rootwork is a form of Hoodoo that concentrates on the fact that every being and object in the universe has a soul and corresponding energies. Successful rootworkers know how to tap into the energies and use them to bring magic and power to their work. The magical tools in Hoodoo simply allow rootworkers to access the natural powers and spiritual intent. They are a medium for blessings and transformations and are part of the process, not the results.

Amulets and charms provide portable vibrations that can be carried or worn by the rootworker.
https://www.pexels.com/photo/nazar-amulets-on-tree-branches-near-stony-formations-in-cappadocia-6243268/

Some cultures and religions believe the same things that Hoodoo followers believe and have named the phenomenon animism. That is the belief that all objects' places and creatures have a distinct essence. The term originated from the Latin word anima, which means "breath of life." Animism teaches us that there are no barriers between the material and spiritual world that cannot be crossed. Hoodoo teaches us the times of the day and year when the veil is at its thinnest and how to use "root" objects to facilitate the connection.

Some people mistake the term "rootworker" as meaning they only work with natural plants and roots. In Hoodoo, the root is the physical home of the spirit and is a sacred place that gives shelter to those spirits that reside there.

How Root Workers Use Items to Symbolize the Powers of the Spirits

1. **Amulets and charms**. These provide portable vibrations that can be carried or worn by the rootworker. They can be ordinary items like keys, coins, and herb bundles that cease to function in their original form. Instead, they become soaked in energy dedicated to creating a specific goal. They become part of a magical process and can be utilized as needed to create a movement in the magical spell. If they are dedicated to soaking up bad energy once the spell has been completed, they are cast out to get rid of the negative energy.

2. **Cashing in on nature's bounty**. Using natural objects is a key part of rootwork, and original practitioners would use the bones of family pets to help with the grieving process and use the residual spirit of the animal to bring good fortune. That wouldn't be as practical today, but you can use the bones of your chicken dinner to recreate the authentic workings of those first rootworkers. If bones aren't your thing, then focus on the natural items all around you and use them instead. Brick dust from red bricks is a powerful protection element; lodestones draw luck, and pyrite attracts good luck. Use nuts, stones, minerals, and herbs in your rootwork to benefit from their powers and spirit.

3. **Poppets** are often mistaken for Voodoo dolls but are much less malignant. They are doll babies that are used to represent individuals or animals in spells. They are generally stuffed with items that belong to the person they represent and additional healing and loving herbs. A Hoodoo doctor baptizes some dolls to name them, while others are kept on altars and shrines. Poppets made for pets will often accompany them to their grave to watch over their spirit and keep them safe.
4. **Personal property.** Using belonging from individuals gives spells an unprecedented level of power. Hair clippings, tears, nails, and bodily fluids are all used in rootwork, while other less personal items include clothing and jewelry. They link the person to the rootworker and direct the magic to the source without any risk of distractions.
5. **Bottles and jars.** In regular kitchens, we know that items in sealed bottles and jars last longer than their shelf life. The same applies to Hoodoo bottles and jars that contain magic. The more durable the container, the longer the spell lasts.

Do Rootworkers Prefer Certain Locations?

Just like the items they work with, the location of their spellwork can be just as effective in their magic. A kitchen is a sacred place at the heart of the home, while their altar and shrine are sacred for different reasons. Crossroads are natural places to perform rituals where two roads meet, or a place where a stream separates into two forks is naturally powerful. Any geographical place that forms a T, X, or Y symbolizes change and is the best place to perform rituals and spells for transformations.

In the past, rootworkers would also gather at gravesides and perform rituals. They would take dirt from the grave and use it in their work. Today we don't see the graveyard as an accepted place for magic. You can visit the graves of your loved ones and ask for advice but limit your work to providing gifts of flowers or stuffed animals to symbolize your love. You don't want to be accused of performing any sort of craft in the graveyard, as that could cause problems.

How to Keep Your Rootwork Pure and Free from Negativity

Cleansing is once more part of your work. It cannot be stated enough that keeping your energy, tools, and roots clean is the most important part of your work. Use these essential washes to clean your home, tools, and feet to ensure your work is pure and successful.

Hoodoo Perfumes and Colognes

Some spiritual practitioners have always made their washes and colognes from scratch, but most Hoodoo workers today buy perfumes from trusted sources. They understand that commercial products are often more powerful since the manufacturers have access to fresher and more available magical ingredients. Some rootworkers will use commercial washes and add their preferred herbs and ingredients for added potency. A little like buying your pizza from the deli and then adding your own toppings to make it even tastier.

- Florida water is considered all-around altar water used to cleanse and protect locations and bring peaceful blessings.
- Hoyt's cologne is used for luck, especially among the gambling communities, and is also a powerful reconciliation scent.
- Kananga water is used in spells to connect to ancestors and in spells for sexual union and increased passion.
- Rose cologne is a gentle-smelling liquid that attracts love and romance, but it can be enhanced with lovage and spikenard to create a more potent cologne.
- Jockey club perfume is especially effective in bringing good luck and improving prosperity.

Washes and Waters for Cleansing

These spiritual supplies are also available for purchase rather than using your homemade potions. They are blessed with herbal and mineral salts imbued with essential oils and concentrated soaps. Some waters are based on a single ingredient, like Rose Water, Orange Water, and Willow water. They allow rootworkers to add their own ingredients and create more potent products.

Spiritual bathing is one of the most traditional rituals in the world. It involves water mixed with Epsom salts and other salt products along with herbs and minerals to provide a cleansing agent for use in the home and personal use. They can remove jinxes and crossed conditions and also draw love and money to practitioners. Rootworkers will also create bath mixtures and sacred soaps for clients and add ingredients that match their needs and desires.

How to Make an Amulet for Your Rootwork

Charms and amulets are perfect for taking your magic on the road. Here are some basic steps to choosing roots that form the perfect amulet for your needs.

Step One: Choose an object that suits the intent you want to set

Your items should be small and durable, especially if they are worn on the body. They should be non-toxic and resistant to wear and tear. Don't forget that your clothing can become a talisman when you bind magic intent in your favorite scarf or tie. Get creative and use your imagination.

Step Two: Cleanse your object

Again, the cleansing ritual should suit the object. Smoke smudging or soapy water will clean most objects and keep them from spiritual infestation.

Step Three: Charge your object

Natural sunlight or moonlight is the easiest way to charge your talismans; just leave them in the beams or rays for a couple of hours. The sun has more masculine associations, while the moon is more feminine. As they charge, add extra energy by chanting or reciting a prayer over them to increase potency.

Step Four: Choose the best time to charge your talisman

We have already covered the ties of the day to set certain intentions, so use those instructions to make your talisman extra powerful.

Once you have created the talisman or charm, wear it on your person or gift it to whoever you made it for. When you gift a root of energy, make sure to explain the power it contains so the wearer will know exactly when to wear it. If the talisman is for a child, sew it into their clothes, or if it is for a pet, put it where they sleep.

Chapter 9: Hoodoo Spells to Enhance Your Life

In this chapter, we will explore how to create spells that will improve your life and give you control over your emotions and energies and the energies surrounding you. Lots of pagan and Wiccan teachings will tell you different methods to do the same thing, but with Hoodoo, you have the resources to gain knowledge and skills from bona fide conjurers and discover their methods so you can improve your own. Earlier in the book, we explored the role of a conjuror and how they would help ordinary folk to benefit from their magic.

When you purchase a spell kit, and the results are favorable, you'll have added to your spiritual repertoire and added knowledge.
https://www.pexels.com/photo/a-person-holding-a-candle-10448633/

Imagine the scene where a fire is burning in a clearing far away from the plantation home, and a group of men, women, and children are seated near the fire with a look of expectancy on their faces. They may be carrying offerings like food or drink, and one by one, they approach a man or woman seated away from the fire. This is a consultation with a conjuror, and they would be given potions, powders, or instructions on how to resolve their issues and enhance their meager lives.

This type of magic was a step up from normal Hoodoo spells, which could be created in the kitchen, and they gave the enslaved people an enhanced feeling of hope that things could get better. They could expect revenge if someone had caused them pain or wronged them. If someone caught their eye, they would be given potions to make them more attractive to the object of their desire.

Today we don't have to consult conjurors and Hoodoo masters to take control of our own lives, but as beginners, it can be handy to have expert help. When you start to practice Hoodoo, the list of ingredients and their corresponding powers can be overwhelming, and using readymade supplies will make your magic easier to access. They provide a source of lucky mojo objects, oils for your baths, and other specific supplies that are safe to use and will expand your knowledge of exactly what Hoodoo can do if you have the knowledge.

The Lucky Mojo Curio Co is an online domain that employs proficient conjurors and skilled Hoodoo rootworkers to produce ready-made products for your use. They provide spell kits with all the ingredients you need and detailed instructions that are perfect for beginners who haven't yet built an herb collection or don't have the other tools a conjuror would have. Their spell kits are a way to test your power of magic without spending a lot of money. When you purchase a spell kit, and the results are favorable, you'll have added to your spiritual repertoire and added knowledge.

The powders and oils they include are pre-blessed and save you the worry of wondering if all your ingredients are effective. You are guaranteed to receive a spell that will work for you providing you use them correctly.

Try these basic spell kits

A Blessing spell kit for less than $60. Use to bless new homes, strengthen new ventures, and heal emotional wounds

- One white crucifix candle
- Blessing bath crystals
- Blessing incense
- Blessing sachets for good luck and love
- Chinese wash
- Lucky mojo bag fixed with oil and containing a dove charm and relevant herbs
- Full instructions for use

A Commanding spell kit costing less than $80 and is used to gain command over others in business, love, and relationships

- Nine yellow candles
- Command bath crystals
- Incense powders
- Sachet powders
- Command Mojo bag sealed with commanding oil and containing relevant herbs and charms
- Full instructions for use

Other spells include a come-to-me spell kit, cast-off evil, a court case spell kit, a crossing spell kit, and a fast luck spell kit.

Depending on your budget and needs, many different Hoodoo resources are available. Check that they are reputable and have good reviews before you make any purchases. Using spell kits isn't cheating or taking the easy route. It simply ensures you enjoy the process before you commit and spend money on your supplies.

Easy Hoodoo Spells for Beginners That Are Simple but Effective

Casting your own spells is a satisfying experience. When you see results, the feeling of power can be overwhelming. Try these simple spells for real results, and start your Hoodoo work with a bang.

The Love Spell for Someone with a Love for Desserts

If your man is losing interest or you want to get closer to a friend and take the next step, make this dessert for them, and make them fall head over heels in love with you.

What You Need
- Hairbrush
- Your favorite scent
- Salt
- Apple pie made with nutmeg and cloves
- Love oil, use rose essential oil or make your own with olive oil and sage or your favored herb

First, brush your hair with the hairbrush with the added love oil, and when you get the chance, brush his hair with the same brush. This improves your connection and plants the seeds of love in his mind.

Next, wash an item of clothing of his along with your bedsheets. As you wash them, chant the following, "*Love me (add name) and feel the soft texture of my sheets as we make love*" seven times over the water as you wash. Dry the sheets and then spray them with your favorite scent as you make the bed. Repeat the same chant another seven times before you fold down the sheets and visualize the two of you beneath the sheets later.

Bake the apple pie or reheat the store-bought one and sprinkle the hot pie with a few drops of your bathwater to get him addicted to you. The cloves will help you command him, and the nutmeg will inspire love.

Ask him to remove his shoes before you serve him the pie and put salt in the shoes to keep him safe from other women's wiles and tricks.

Finally, add some of your sexual fluids to your lipstick. Then, if you do kiss, it will drive him crazy with lust and bind him to you forever.

Honey Jar Spells

Honey is one of the most common ingredients in Hoodoo spells because it is the epitome of sweetness and attracts the people you want in your life, and because it is so sticky, it keeps them there. Honey has strong connections with the goddess of love, Aphrodite, and other prominent love deities. A jar of honey is the perfect way to bind your intentions and keep the herbs that power your spell fresh and potent.

Try this binding honey jar to keep someone you love close to you

What You Need

- A jar of honey
- Pen and paper
- Herbs
- Love oil
- Red candle
- Lighter

Take the paper and write the name of the person you wish to bind across the page. Turn the paper ninety degrees and write your name. Repeat the process until you have a multilayered representation of your two names. Now create a circle of words representing your love around the names without lifting the pen from the paper. Write "I love you, stay with me" or your own phrase to create a binding circle of love.

Add your chosen herbs to the paper and add any personal fluids or items from the two of you. These can be fingernails, hair, or fluids from your body. The choice is yours. Now anoint the paper with the love oil and add to the honey jar.

Charge your jar with additional items and herbs to create a powerful environment for your petition. Add cinnamon for lust, saffron for passion, and cardamom for loyalty. Lodestones and rose petals will make your honey even more potent.

As you close and seal the jar, repeat the phrase, *"Bless this honey that is sweet to me (add the name of your desired partner). I ask that you also show your love and share the sweet love we both can be."* Repeat three times and then seal the jar by burning the red candle on the lid of the jar.

Banishing Powder for Protection

Keeping your home and your family safe is one of the most important spells you can cast. Creating this powder will help you banish evil spirits and keep negativity from your energies.

What You Need

- Dried lemon peel
- Osha root

- Dried garlic
- Salt

Take equal parts of all the ingredients and grind them with a pestle and mortar while reciting your favorite Bible passage or mantra for protection. *"Bring your powerful protection to my life and keep us safe from all harm."*

Hoodoo Happiness Spell

When you need some joy in your life, try this simple spell to bring happiness and love

What You Need

- Three orange or yellow candles
- Cedar oil
- A couple of pinches of rosemary
- A pinch of marjoram

Anoint all the candles with your oil, and then dress the candle with your herbs. Place them in holders on your shrine or altar and stare at the flames as you repeat this mantra,

"Bring joy and love to me and mine,
Banish anger and stress, let go of strife,
I am happy, and I am free
I won't stand for negativity."

Hold your hands over the flames and feel the warmth they give off without burning your hands. Visualize the happiness and love that is about to come into your life as the candles burn away naturally. Take the remnants of the candles, place them in a yellow cloth bag with more rosemary and marjoram, and place the bag beneath your bed.

New Beginnings Spell

This spell is perfect for New Year's resolutions or whenever you need to eliminate negative elements of your life. It helps you to move on and escape any negative energies. This spell is for moving on from parts of your life rather than a specific person.

What You Need

- Two sprigs of rosemary
- A dried stick of wood around the size of your ring finger

- Black yarn
- White yarn
- Heatproof pot
- Large spoon
- White candle
- Black candle

Use the black yarn to tie one piece of rosemary to the stick and the white yarn to tie the remaining sprig to the opposite end. Lay this down and place a black candle to the left and a white candle to the right. Light the black candle and state to the room what you intend to leave behind. Now light the white candle and state to the room what you hope to attract to your life to fill the gap.

Lift the stick so the black yarn is above the black candle and the white yarn is over the white candle. Don't let the stick catch fire. Hold it high enough to avoid the flames. Now, snap the stick in half and cast it into the awaiting pot. Hold your hands over the flames and repeat the intentions you stated in the first part of the spell. Bring the pot between the two candles and bang it sharply three times with the spoon to release the energy from the stick.

You have now made the break, so let the candles burn down naturally, and add the wax to the broken stick and twine. Take the remnants to a place that is far from your home and dispose of them safely, preferably in running water or fire.

Money Spell

When casting money spells, the key thing to remember is that they will not reward greed. They are only effective in times of need and when your intentions are genuine. Ask for wealth and prosperity by all means, but it may not result in cold hard cash. After all, a happy life isn't necessarily based on your monetary worth.

Pay a Bill Spell

This is an example of how your Hoodoo magic can be used to pay a specific bill in times of hardship.

What You Need
- Green candle
- Cinnamon oil

- The incense that compliments the oil
- Paper and pen

Take the pen and create a representation of the bill you need to pay. **You will be burning it, so don't use the original!** Use words and images to create a strong and detailed idea of the bill. Making your own drawing will create personal energy rather than just using a photocopy of the original.

Anoint and dress the candle with your chosen oil and light your incense. Place the folded paper under the candle holder and repeat the following,

> "As the candle burns away,
> The light of the spirits lights my day,
> They bring the cash that I need
> So I can pay this bill at speed."

Concentrate on the bill and how it will feel to get it paid while the candle burns for ten minutes. Snuff out the candle and leave the area. Return the next day and repeat the process. Do the same until the candle has only one day left to burn. Take the paper and burn it in the remaining flame of the candle. Any unexpected money that comes your way must be put toward paying this bill. If you don't, the spirits will get angry and make sure you don't benefit from their help again.

Fertility Spell

If a young couple is struggling to become pregnant and all the health options have been followed, Hoodoo can bring that extra fertility boost to their lives and give Mother Nature a helping hand.

This spell is used at harvest time to bring a good crop to the fields, but it is also a powerful fertility spell.

What You Need

- Patchouli oil
- Sandalwood incense
- To dried pinecones
- Five grains of wheat
- Green candle
- Paper and a green pen

- Cooking pot

Take the paper and write the name of the child you want to conceive in green. Don't worry if you don't have a name in your mind. This is just a symbol of the child you hope will come to you. Anoint the candle with the oil and light the incense. Add the wheat and pinecones to the paper in the cooking pot. Light the paper with your candle as you imagine your child and what they will mean to you. Once the flames have died down, let the remnants cool before burying them in your yard or another personal space.

The Buried Egg Spell

What You Need

- An egg
- Whole vanilla pod
- Green marker
- Plant pot and soil

Take the egg and decorate it to represent your child. Use symbols and a name to create the representation of your desire. Take the pot and soil and bury the egg beneath the soil. Place the pot in your sacred space and water it every night while you say a mantra over the pot.

> *"Sacred egg grow and flourish,*
> *Let the earth be your womb,*
> *Bring that power to my body*
> *And let my child be born."*

Ensure the pot is drained properly, and concentrate all your intentions with your nightly watering.

These are just a few spells to bring abundance and love to your life. It would be impossible to list them all, but it does give you some ideas for your early work. Remember, your intentions are the fuel that powers your spells, so keep them at the forefront of your mind and always be true to yourself.

Chapter 10: Living a Hoodoo Lifestyle

Once you have experienced the joy and wonder that Hoodoo can bring to your life, some people believe the next step is to live a daily routine to incorporate their new powers into their regular life. This doesn't mean you become a witch doctor or abandon your regular job and social life to concentrate on your magic. It just means you use the things you are learning to enhance your life and make your own decisions. You are on the path to gaining control of your destiny, and you will use all your Hoodoo knowledge to live your best life.

Create a journal for your thoughts and use it to get creative and list your wildest dreams.
https://www.pexels.com/photo/white-notebook-and-pen-606539/

Did you know that the spoken word is responsible for around 8% of communication? The most significant way to communicate with the universe and the spirits is to use every method of stating your intentions by living a life filled with purpose. Raise your energy and vibrations to fill your life with positivity, and then begin to receive the rewards.

State Your Intentions in Written Form

We have already established that the only way to get what you want is to ask for it clearly and to choose ingredients for your work that signal your needs. Create a journal for your thoughts and use it to get creative and list your wildest dreams. A journal can be uplifting, and you should fill it with images, words, and mantras that will state your intentions and remind you daily what you want, need, and deserve.

Tips for Keeping a Journal

So, you have your brand-new journal and your set of pens, and you are faced with that spotless first page. What do you do for your first journaling experience? Even avid journal keepers can be intimidated by a new project and get those page jitters. Don't be overwhelmed; follow these tips, and get journaling.

1. Make your first page a statement about yourself. Add a picture and some details about yourself. Writing about yourself will get your creative juices flowing and settle those nerves. Write what you know, and that first page will soon be filled with glorious details and information.

2. Create a prompt list for your day. The journal is for recording your feelings and your thoughts, but what should you be recording? Prompt lists help you start to use journaling regularly and get you into the habit of recording your thoughts.

    Here are some prompts you could use:

    - List ten things that take you to your happy place.
    - What are the three things you can't live without?
    - What three habits do you have this year that you don't want to carry into next year?
    - Write about the best experience you had last year and how you felt.

- Now do the same for the worst experience from last year.
- Divide yourself into three sections, your body, mind, and soul. What does it feel like to be that part of you, and how can you make each part feel better?
- Who are you? In ten words, describe yourself and then ask your most trusted friend to do the same and compare how similar or different the lists are.
- List all the areas of your life you want to change and how starting with finances and health and then dealing with your emotional needs.
- What sort of class would you like to take, just for fun and not to improve your career?

You get the idea. Having a chat with yourself can be so revealing, and when you have the powers of Hoodoo on your side, you feel like you can actually make these changes.

Become More Mindful

Stop thinking that mindfulness is just for hippy-dippy people and start to understand exactly what mindfulness involves. Exercises to increase your mindfulness help you reach a heightened state of awareness and increased happiness. You will feel less stressed and more aware of the benefits of your surroundings. When you are mindful, you'll start to appreciate the grass that grows beneath your feet and the sky that contains the sun and the moon.

Just doing a couple of mindfulness exercises will help you raise your vibrations and become more in tune with the world. Incorporate these into your life, and you'll immediately begin to feel the benefits of your change of pace.

Create a Morning Routine
Shower

Having a routine when you wake avoids that feeling of despair some of us feel when we first wake. You know what to do and when. Start the day with a mindful shower and feel the water hitting you and the warmth it brings. Feel the texture of the soapy bubbles or creamy lather from your shower gel, and watch how it travels down your body. Finish the experience with a blast of icy water to reawaken your senses and close your pores. That tingling sensation sets you up for the day.

Have a Drink and a Light Breakfast

Start your day with a boost of energy with an energy-packed breakfast. We will cover foods and what they bring to you later. Choose a drink that peps you up, like tasty herbal tea or a cup of coffee, decaffeinated possibly. These simple ingredients will keep you alert until your next meal, so make sure they contain the energy you need.

Move That Body

Stretch your muscles to avoid any cramping before you leave the house. Bending and touching your toes limbs you up, but if you can manage more strenuous exercises, go for it. A couple of star jumps and press-ups are easy to do in any environment. If you feel like you need to take in some fresh air, go for a run or a power walk around the block. Whenever possible, ditch your car and walk to work or the shops to keep your environment cleaner and improve your fitness. You will function better in all areas of your life, including your magic.

Use Your Waiting Time Effectively

How much of your life is spent waiting for other people or for something to happen? What is your normal mental state when waiting? Frustration? Anger? Boredom? Chances are you don't use this time constructively because chances are if you try and get something done, it will be interrupted by the event you are waiting for. Next time you hang on for a zoom call or are in line in the coffee shop waiting for your drink, change how you use this time.

Use your full range of senses to notice your surroundings more. What can you hear? Coffee cups clinking and general chatter or the hum of the air conditioning would normally be ignored. When you are waiting for a call, notice the surroundings you are in and become engaged with the environment. You will soon start to enjoy waiting and see it as a positive action rather than getting frustrated and fretful.

Connect to the Earth Mindfully

This practice will help you in your grounding following Hoodoo work, so improving your technique will make sure you keep your energy fields balanced and in tune with the earth. Whenever you can connect with nature by closing your eyes and noticing the breeze on your face and the warmth of the sun as it hits your skin. Walk barefoot on the grass and feel the energy of the earth flow through your body and energize your spirit. Whenever you can connect to natural elements, swim in the sea, climb a hill or mountain and have a campfire in the great outdoors.

Mindful Eating

We will look more carefully at the foods we eat and what they bring later, but have you ever considered how you eat as well as what you eat? Do you appreciate your food, or do you just eat and forget? Why do you eat? Are you genuinely hungry, or could it be boredom? When you change the way you eat, you change your attitude toward food and learn to recognize genuine hunger rather than other responses that trigger you to eat.

1. **Mindful beverages**. When you drink something, take the time to notice every taste in the liquid. Is there a hint of lemon in your tea, or is it infused with mint? Is your coffee freshly ground or instant? What is the difference, and how does it affect your tastebuds? Do you drink too much coffee, and are your taste buds incapable of distinguishing quality? Cut down the amount you have and improve the quality instead.

2. **Mindful eating**. When you consume food, do you appreciate every mouthful or shovel your food down simply to fuel your body? Take the time to appreciate the texture of your food and how it feels on your tongue. Is it crunchy, or is it soft and squishy? How does your food smell? Bring it up to your nose and appreciate the aromas you experience before you eat it and during the meal. What emotional triggers do you feel when you eat? How do you feel during the meal, and how do you feel after it is finished?

3. **Listen to your food**. Using all your senses is part of life, but when you concentrate on the food, you can block out all other sensual triggers. Listen to the bubbles in your carbonated drink and enjoy the sound. Does your food make a sound on the plate? What are the sounds that surround the table? If you are in a restaurant, can you hear the sounds of the kitchen or listen to the other guests?

Mindfulness is an art that can be practiced anywhere and by anyone. It takes practice but is a part of life that cannot be ignored. You may be wondering what mindfulness and Hoodoo have in common, and the answer is simple. Once you understand the basics of mindfulness, you'll see the connection. We constantly strive for a heightened spiritual connection, and mindfulness is all about strengthening that energy. Imagine visiting a celebrated art gallery packed to the brim with artworks from the greatest artists that ever lived, and all you are looking at is the floor. Raise your eyes and appreciate the wonders of the natural world, and you'll soon feel the connection.

Mojo Bags

You already know the power of your mojo bag and what the different colored bags mean. How many times do you take one with you as you leave home for the day? If you leave them behind, they will charge themselves on your altar or shrine, but they won't serve your needs in the regular world. Your bags should be a part of your normal dressing routine. Try sewing an internal pocket on some of your favorite items of clothing to make a place for your bag. This way, you can keep it close to your skin and avoid it falling out and creating interest you may not want.

Your mojo bag is the ultimate accessory to carry with you and bring magic to your life. Picking it up should come as naturally as taking your house keys and your phone. You should feel like it is a natural extension of your personality and always carry one with you.

Food and Drink

Now for the tasty stuff. Hoodoo practitioners should follow a healthy diet to keep their spirit and body strong and ready for their workings. Stamina and clarity of thought help you get the best results and improve your magic powers.

Traditional Hoodoo Food

One of the best ways you can honor the memory of the original Hoodoo workers is to make their food and revel in the taste and traditions of the African American culture. Soul food is a generic term that covers some of the classic dishes that have been passed down through the generations to become the dishes we know today.

Nobody is suggesting that you completely change your diet to soul food. That would be unsustainable and possibly unhealthy, but having soul food on special occasions will help you connect to your roots and recognize how the dishes signify the struggle they faced for survival. Enslavers gave their enslaved people the bare minimum of ingredients, and their rations were low in nutrition and often inferior. The masters failed to recognize that if they fed their enslaved people better quality food, they would thrive and become more productive. Today we consider soul food a source of comfort and decadence when, in reality, it originated from the creativity it took to turn basic ingredients into tasty and sustainable food.

Rice

Few people know that before the slave trade era, rice wasn't generally available in the US. The traders who imported enslaved people from Africa would often take crops native to Africa aboard the ships the enslaved people occupied. They used the crops to keep the occupants alive, and on arrival in the US, they planted the crops on plantations and became part of US food over time.

The two cultures came together to create fabulous one-pot recipes like Jollof and jambalaya that are popular today and give a snapshot into the early cuisine of African American folks.

Jambalaya

Try this Creole version for a hearty dish that is simple to make and delicious

Ingredients

- 1 lb. boneless chicken thighs diced and sliced
- 6oz spicy sausage
- 1 lb. medium-sized shrimp, cleaned and deveined
- I packet of long-grain rice
- Two cloves of garlic
- One can of tomatoes
- Two cups of chicken stock
- Two tbsp. tomato puree
- One white onion

- Two green onions
- Two bell peppers
- Himalayan salt
- Black pepper
- One tsp oregano
- One tbsp. olive oil

Instructions:
1. In a large saucepan, heat the oil, add the chicken peppers, onions, and seasoning, and cook for five minutes until the chicken is browned.
2. Add the spicy sausage, the garlic, and the tomato puree, and cook until it smells amazing.
3. Now add the chicken stock, tinned tomatoes, and rice to the pot.
4. Lower the heat on the stove, place a tight lid on the pot, and let it simmer for twenty minutes.
5. When the rice is tender, add the shrimp and cook for three to five minutes until they turn pink.
6. Add the green onions for crunch and serve immediately.

BBQ Pork

As you would expect, the cuts of pork given to slaves weren't the best, and they had to mask the poor flavor of the meat with sauces using their African cooking knowledge to make spectacular combinations that flavored and moistened the pork.

Try these sauces to coat your pork

Black BBQ sauce
Ingredients
- ¼ cup chopped onion
- ½ cup of distilled white vinegar
- ¼ cup soy sauce or Worcester sauce
- 2 tbsp. brown sugar
- 2 tsp lemon juice
- ¼ teaspoon black pepper

- ¼ tsp Tabasco sauce
- A pinch of coarse salt
- 2 tsp olive oil

Instructions:
1. In a solid base pan, heat the oil and add the onions, and fry until they have softened.
2. Add the rest of the ingredients and simmer for fifteen minutes with the lid off.
3. Wait until the sauce has thickened, and take it off the heat.
4. Serve warm or cold as an accompaniment, or baste your meat in the sauce for four hours before cooking.

What do you notice about the sauce that makes it stand out from other BBQ sauces? No tomatoes. Vinegar was a key part of early African American cooking as it was cheap and effective at tenderizing meat and made the sauce tangy rather than sweet.

Greens

Collard greens and boiled leafy green dishes are a staple part of soul food, and the liquid left behind after boiling the vegetables was added to any leftover fat from the pork, seasoned, and named "potlikker." The slaves would then bake cornbread and use it to soak up the juices as a filling snack.

Chitlins

Commonly referred to as chitterlings, these tasty dishes are based on the intestines of the domestic pig or cows filled with whatever was lying around in the kitchen stuffed into the pot and boiled or fried. They have a distinctly meaty flavor and aren't for the faint-hearted. If you do want to try the dish, ask your butcher to clean and prepare the pig's intestines for safety reasons. If you don't clean them properly, you can cause serious illnesses that will last for weeks.

However, professionally prepared chitlins can be easily sourced. Once you have them, the rest of the dish is all about what you have to hand. Add the chitlins to a large cooking pot and add garlic, apple, vinegar, pepper, salt, and any other ingredient you think will make the dish tasty. Boil for two hours to ensure the chitterlings are cooked, and let the mixture rest before pouring it through a colander.

Take the cooked chitlins and dry them with a clean cloth. Make a batter from flour and water with seasoning. Heat oil in a frying pan and coat the chitlins in batter before frying until they are golden and crisp. Place them on kitchen paper to drain before you season and eat them. Enjoy your soul food.

Sweet Potato Pie

Sweet potatoes are a traditional ingredient in soul food and are delicious as a side dish or cooked in this tasty pie.

Ingredients

- 1 9" uncooked pie shell
- Three medium sweet potatoes
- Two eggs
- ½ cup full-fat milk
- 600g unsalted butter
- One ¼ cup of white sugar
- One tbsp flour
- One tbsp. lemon juice
- One tbsp. nutmeg

Instructions:

1. Boil the unpeeled sweet potatoes in water until you can pierce the skin with a fork; around twenty minutes should work.
2. Let them cool before peeling and mashing the flesh.
3. Add the butter, sugar, flour, milk, eggs, and nutmeg, and mix well.
4. Add the mixture to the uncooked shell and place in preheated oven for thirty minutes.

Foods That Will Improve Your Spiritual Balance and Raise Your Vibrations

Your overall diet should be focused on providing you with the best ingredients possible to make your body work and boost your mind and spirit.

Incorporate these foods into your diet to make a significant difference to your health and your spirituality:

Fatty Fish

Fatty and oily fish are packed with essential oils that stimulate your brain and contribute to the fluidity of your brain's membrane. They contain essential omega-3 acids that combat depression and boost the development of hormones that lift your mood. Eat a portion of salmon or tuna twice a week to make sure you get the correct amount of these nutrients in your diet.

Dark Chocolate

Chocolate may not seem viable for your diet, but it is filled with mind-boosting components that release substances that boost your mood and raise your psychological response to eating it. Regular chocolate has elevated sugar and fat levels, so choose a darker option to benefit from the flavonoids and lower sugar levels. A small square every three days should provide you with the benefits and avoid the calories.

Fermented Foods

If you have taken a close look at the dairy section in your local store, chances are you have spotted fermented products like kimchi and kefir among the more regular yogurt options. Fermenting allows the growth of natural bacteria that functions in your gut to increase serotonin levels and improve your mood, raise your sex drive, and lessen stress levels. Try foods that are rich in probiotics and improve your gut function significantly.

Bananas

These tropical fruits may seem ordinary at first, but they are a healthy source of fiber known as prebiotics. This fiber works in your gut to slowly release sugar into your bloodstream to avoid mood swings and depression. They are packed with vitamin B6, which releases dopamine and serotonin, the most effective feel-good transmitters. One large banana every week will keep your blood sugar levels healthy and your mood stable.

Oats

Whole grains are a major source of fiber and are packed with iron. Just one cup of raw oats has 81g of iron which is 20% of your daily needs. These healthy doses of iron help combat sluggishness and raise energy levels.

Fruit and Vegetables

A diet filled with fresh ingredients is obviously better for you than processed ingredients, but it isn't always achievable. You can stick to seasonal ingredients in your food choices to make sure you get fresh ingredients all year round, but frozen fruit and veg can be just as nutritious if cooked correctly. Choose fruit high in antioxidants, like berries, to boost your energy levels, and fight disease.

Keep yourself hydrated and choose fresh ingredients whenever you can; organic and wild options are also better for you but can prove more expensive. You know the value of a good diet and how it helps you function at an optimum level, so budget for a better diet, and you'll soon see the difference.

Timing Is Everything in Hoodoo Rituals

Knowing when to perform rituals is an art that is part of your learned knowledge. A lot of your work is based on instinctively knowing what works for you, but the "good and bad" hours are part of your research. Timing will help you bring the intention to your work and make your rituals and spells more effective.

The time of day you cast your spells or perform your ritual adds certain strengths to your work, so it is worth familiarizing yourself with these correspondences.

Sunrise is all about power

Casting spells at sunrise helps you shine light onto darkness and is perfect for new beginnings and new love. Rituals for healing and friendship should be performed at sunrise – and any spells that include financial and career matters. Working in the sunrise will enhance your spiritual connections as you bathe in the first light of the day.

Noon magic is all about amplification

Noon is the balanced hour of the day and the perfect time to banish unhealthy habits and dispel toxicity from your life. It amplifies your intent and ensures the negativity you seek to get rid of is gone as the noon hour passes. Spells for drawing success and love will be strengthened if you start your ritual before noon and finish it at the end.

Sunset spells and rituals are all about saying goodbye

When you are ready to release old aspects of your life, the best time to do so is at sunset. Intentions should include banishments, healing from toxicity, peace, and rest. If you want to bury any remnants from your banishing spells, it is wise to bury them in the west so the sun will set on them every day and ensure the intentions remain in the ground.

Midnight is the time for energy spells and rituals

It is the wakening hour for the spiritual world, and as the clock hands move toward midnight, it is the time for growing intentions, and as it passes the midnight hour, it is time for releasing them. Banishing spells should begin before midnight and finish just after.

Witching hour

Folklore states that the hour between 3 am and 4 am is the Devil's hour and a time for paranormal activity. If you do find yourself awake at the witching hour, cast a circle of protection, take some divination tools, and throw them down just to see what happens. Who knows, you may have a message sent to you through the veil that separates the physical and spiritual world when it is at its thinnest.

The Days of the Week and How They Affect Your Spells and Rituals

Sunday magic

Best for prosperity and strength, vitality, healing, and financial victories.

Monday magic

Best for love, healing, psychic connections, and friendship. Perform shadow and spirit work to enhance your dreams and emotional balance.

Tuesday magic

Best for legal matters, protection, courage, and confidence. Rituals should be performed for power and passion and to reverse any spells that have been cast against you.

Wednesday magic

Best for communication, divination, clarity of thought, spiritual enlightenment, wisdom, and knowledge.

Thursday magic

Best for good luck, especially in legal and business matters, fiscal growth, career moves, health, and political matters.

Friday magic

Best for love and passion. Also, a powerful day for all female magic like fertility and household matters, beauty, and love.

Saturday's magic

Best for self-improvement and transformation. Use Saturday to perform rituals for liberation and banishing unpleasant habits.

Taking Hoodoo Baths

No matter what the day of the week or the work you have done, you'll always benefit from a bath to set your intentions and heal any parts of your energy or physical self that your magic work may have drained. Try these specialized baths to energize and relax you at the same time.

These recipes are for baths that will solve any issues and bring positivity to your spirit.

Purification Bath

If you feel weighed down by some emotional or physical matters, this bath will release any negative energy and release your anxiety. This bath will also ease any flu or cold symptoms.

- Three cups of evaporated milk
- 3 tbsp. anise
- Sprinkling of rue
- A bowl of sea salt
- Two white candles
- Coconut incense

Instructions:

1. Draw a hot bath and add the milk, anise, and rue. Swirl the water until it forms a milky bath.

2. Light the two white candles and place them at the head of the bath before you lie in it.
3. Now take the bowl of salt and wash yourself from your head to your feet with a gentle exfoliating motion.
4. Once you have finished, let yourself relax in the water until you feel relaxed and cleansed.
5. When you leave the bath, dab yourself dry with a clean towel.

The Yellow Bath for Attraction

Do you need to get your relationship in order or attract a new love? Try this attraction bath if you need to attract any form of passion, love, or friendship. It is also good for skin ailments like dry skin or psoriasis.

- Yellow food coloring
- Yarrow flowers
- Parsley
- Citrine crystals
- Lemon incense
- Yellow and white candle
- Honey-based body scrub

Instructions:

1. Draw the bath with the yarrow and parsley and add the food coloring.
2. Light the candles and place the crystal at the head of the bathtub.
3. Gently wash yourself with the body scrub until your skin tingles.
4. If you have a person in mind you want to attract, try visualizing them or saying their name aloud.
5. You can use natural honey to wash but be warned. It will get sticky.

Spiritual Bath for Complete Refreshment and Clarification

Sometimes you just need a thorough clear-out, both mentally and physically. This bath will refresh your body and soul.

- One cup rainwater
- Coconut water
- Rice water
- Dried milk powder
- Egg white
- Three white candles

Instructions:
1. Draw your bath as usual and add all the ingredients except the candles.
2. Place the candles at the head of the bath and light them.
3. Soak yourself for twenty minutes and submerge your head in the bath at least twice.
4. Relax and feel the stress and worry flow out of you and into the ether.

Money Bath

Try this bath whenever you need to improve your financial status or attract fast cash. It is also effective in promoting good luck in business and gambling.

- Red clover
- Rose petals
- Calendula
- Chamomile
- Three green candles
- A jade crystal

Instructions:
1. Add all the ingredients to a hot bath except the candles and jade.
2. Place the candles at the head of the bath and put the crystal at the foot of the middle candle.
3. Sit in the bath and relax while you visualize your new future filled with wealth and prosperity.

Of course, these are just a few ideas for your Hoodoo baths. Take a look at the ingredients chapter to inspire you with ingredients to set your intention. Remember that some ingredients may cause skin irritation, and you should only use items that are safe in the water.

Conclusion

Now you have the knowledge, the instructions, and hopefully the passion for your new life as a Hoodoo practitioner. Are you excited? You should be. This was the first step in a whole new universe filled with everything you need to make your life become filled with your every desire. Hoodoo is a community of people who love to share their stories and experiences, and as you become more immersed in the magic, you'll become a willing member of this community. Sharing skills and new discoveries will become second nature to you, and the joy you get from your work will grow with your experience.

Good luck on your journey, and congratulations, you are now Hoodoo-ready!

Here's another book by Silvia Hill that you might like

Free Bonus from Silvia Hill available for limited time

Hi Spirituality Lovers!

My name is Silvia Hill, and first off, I want to THANK YOU for reading my book.

Now you have a chance to join my exclusive spirituality email list so you can get the ebooks below for free as well as the potential to get more spirituality ebooks for free! Simply click the link below to join.

P.S. Remember that it's 100% free to join the list.

~~$27~~ **FREE BONUSES**

- 9 Types of Spirit Guides and How to Connect to Them
- How to Develop Your Intuition: 7 Secrets for Psychic Development and Tarot Reading
- Tarot Reading Secrets for Love, Career, and General Messages

Access your free bonuses here
https://livetolearn.lpages.co/hoodoo-for-beginners-paperback/

References

"10 Mojo Bag Color Meanings Explained [+ How to Use Them]." *Magickalspot.com*, 19 Sept. 2020, https://magickalspot.com/mojo-bag-colors/

"A List of Powerful Herbs for Love Spells [+Zodiac Signs]." *Magickalspot.com*, 5 May 2020, https://magickalspot.com/herbs-for-love-spells/ .

americanadmin. "Facts about High John the Conqueror." *American History for Kids*, 24 July 2019, www.americanhistoryforkids.com/the-civil-war-high-john-the-conqueror/.

Ashley, Kelly. "10 Signs You Need to Clear Your Energy Now." *Spiritual Awakening Signs*, 19 Jan. 2019, https://spiritualawakeningsigns.com/spiritualawakening/10-signs-you-need-to-clear-your-energy-now/#:~:text=So%2C%20with%20that%20in%20mind%2C%20here%20are%2010

Bird, Stephanie Rose. "10 Tips to Help You Practice 365 Days of Hoodoo." *Llewellyn Worldwide*, 3 Dec. 2018, www.llewellyn.com/journal/article/2718 .

"Bottle Trees: A Beautiful Tradition with a Spiritual Past." *HowStuffWorks*, 5 Oct. 2022, https://history.howstuffworks.com/history-vs-myth/bottle-tree.htm .

Fertility Spells - Free Witchcraft Spells. https://freewitchspells.com/fertility-spells

fields. "Candle Magic for Beginners: Your ULTIMATE Guide." *Otherworldly Oracle*, 23 Oct. 2018, https://otherworldlyoracle.com/candle-magic-for-beginners/ .

"How to Connect with Your Ancestors in 10 EFFECTIVE Ways." *Otherworldly Oracle*, 13 Mar. 2019, https://otherworldlyoracle.com/how-to-connect-with-your-ancestors/ .

"Spiritual Cleansing: Your Guide to Cleansing Rituals and Methods." *Otherworldly Oracle*, 8 July 2019, https://otherworldlyoracle.com/spiritual-cleansing-rituals/ .

Hayford, Vanessa. "The Humble History of Soul Food • BLACK FOODIE." *Black Foodie*, 22 Jan. 2018, www.blackfoodie.co/the-humble-history-of-soul-food/ .

Hayn, Lyza. "Spiritual Meaning of the Kongo Cosmogram (Dikenga)." *OutofStress.com*, 14 Oct. 2022, www.outofstress.com/kongo-cosmogram-spiritual-meaning/#:~:text=The%20Kongo%20Cosmogram%20%28also%20known%20as%20Dikenga%20or .

Heckman, William. "12 Fun Mindfulness Exercises." *The American Institute of Stress*, 10 Feb. 2021, www.stress.org/12-fun-mindfulness-exercises .

"Hoodoo Formulas and Recipes." *Www.Hoodoo-Conjure.com*, www.Hoodoo-conjure.com/recipes/bitterbaths.htm .

Hoodoo Herbs - HoodooWitch. 24 Apr. 2016, https://Hoodoowitch.net/book-of-shadows/magickal-Hoodoo-herbs/ .

"Magical Days of the Week: Correspondences & Daily Energy." *Otherworldly Oracle*, 22 Apr. 2020, https://otherworldlyoracle.com/magical-days-of-the-week/ .

"Mojo Bags - What They Are and How to Make Them." *A Pagan Mess*, 27 Jan. 2019, https://apaganmess.com/mojo-bags/#:~:text=How%20to%20Make%2C%20feed%2C%20and%20charge%20mojo%20bags .

"Mood Food: 9 Foods That Can Really Boost Your Spirits." *Healthline*, 5 Feb. 2020, www.healthline.com/nutrition/mood-food#6.-Berries .

Patterson, Rachel. "Hoodoo Herbs and Roots." *Rachelpatterson*, 11 Aug. 2017, www.rachelpatterson.co.uk/single-post/2017/08/11/Hoodoo-Herbs-and-Roots .

"Reading Candle Wax | Divination." *Shirleytwofeathers.com*, https://shirleytwofeathers.com/The_Blog/divination/ceromancy-reading-candle-wax/#:~:text=Another%20way%20to%20observe%20and%20identify%20the%20messages .

"What Is Hoodoo-Conjure." *Theconjureman*, https://theconjureman.com/What_is_Hoodoo-Conjure.html#:~:text=Conjure%2FHoodoo%20is%20a%20form%20of%20folk%20magick%20and .

WiseWitch. "7 Steps for Making Magical Charms, Amulets, Talismans & Fetishes." *Wise Witches and Witchcraft*, 17 Apr. 2018, https://witchcraftandwitches.com/magic-magick/7-steps-for-making-magical-charms-amulets-talismans-fetishes/ .

"Hoodoo Witch (Rootworker)." *Wise Witches and Witchcraft*, 18 Feb. 2018, https://witchcraftandwitches.com/types-of-witches/Hoodoo-witch-rootworker/ .

Wright, Mackenzie Sage. "How to Cast a Jar Spell: Witchcraft for Beginners." *Exemplore*, https://exemplore.com/wicca-witchcraft/Witchcraft-for-Beginners-How-to-Cast-a-Jar-Spell .

"How to Make Your Own Hidden/Portable Shrine." *Exemplore*, exemplore.com/wicca- https://witchcraft/How-to-Make-Your-Own-HiddenPortable-Shrine#gid=ci026e24709000245f&pid=how-to-make-your-own-hiddenportable-shrine-MTc1MTE3NTAwODQ4NTQ2OTEx .

www.ingramcontent.com/pod-product-compliance
Lightning Source LLC
Chambersburg PA
CBHW070337010526
44107CB00004B/537